The Bedevilment of
Elizabeth Lorentz

The Bedevilment of Elizabeth Lorentz

EDITED BY PETER A. MORTON

TRANSLATED BY BARBARA DÄHMS

UNIVERSITY OF TORONTO PRESS

Toronto Buffalo London

Library and Archives Canada Cataloguing in Publication

The bedevilment of Elizabeth Lorentz / edited by Peter A. Morton
    and translated by Barbara Dähms.

Includes bibliographical references and index.
Issued in print and electronic formats.

ISBN 978-1-4426-3491-6 (softcover).—ISBN 978-1-4426-3492-3 (hardcover).
ISBN 978-1-4426-3493-0 (HTML).—ISBN 978-1-4426-3494-7 (PDF).

    1. Lorentz, Elizabeth, 1647—Trials, litigation, etc.   2. Demoniac possession—Germany—Case studies.   3. Women servants—Germany–Biography.   4. Reformation—Germany.
I. Dähms, Barbara, 1954–, translator.   I. Morton, Peter A. (Peter Alan), 1952–, editor.

BT975.B43 2018   133.4'26092   C2018-903459-9
                                                 C2018-903460-2

We welcome comments and suggestions regarding any aspect of our publications – please feel free to contact us at news@utorontopress.com or visit our Internet site at utorontopress.com.

North America
5201 Dufferin Street NBN International
North York, Ontario, Canada, M3H 5T8

2250 Military Road
Tonawanda, New York, USA, 14150

orders phone: 1-800-565-9523
orders fax: 1-800-221-9985
orders e-mail: utpbooks@utpress.utoronto.ca

UK, Ireland, and continental Europe
NBN International
Estover Road, Plymouth, PL6 7PY, UK

orders phone: 44 (0) 1752 202301
orders fax: 44 (0) 1752 202333
orders e-mail: enquiries@nbninternational.com

University of Toronto Press acknowledges the financial assistance to its publishing program of the Canada Council for the Arts and the Ontario Arts Council, an agency of the Government of Ontario.

Printed in the United States of America.

To Christian Hogrefe
for his kindness over the years.

Contents

Illustrations

Acknowledgments

We thank the staff of the Stadtarchiv Braunschweig, especially the director Hennig Steinführer, for their assistance with the trial records, which are in their possession. Much of the work for the Introduction was completed at the Herzog August Bibliothek in Wolfenbüttel, and we thank the staff of the library for their continuous assistance and support. Jill Bepler of the Herzog August Bibliothek has been tremendously helpful over the years, as has Christian Hogrefe, to whom this book is dedicated.

We thank three anonymous reviewers for their thoughtful commentaries and their suggestions for the manuscript. The book has benefitted much from their work. Jeffrey Suderman read an early version of the manuscript and gave it a much-improved direction. For translations of the Latin we had help from Damaris Aschera Gehr, Burghard Schmank, and Asaph Ben-Tov; if errors remain in those translations, they are our own. We thank the pastor of the Church of St. Peter in Brunswick, Gabriele Geyer-Knüppel, for a lovely conversation about Melchior Neukirch and a tour of her church. Tania Therien, the copy-editor, did a wonderful job, and we are grateful for her attention to detail. Finally, we thank Natalie Fingerhut of the University of Toronto Press, first for her suggestion that we consider doing a second book for the press, and then for her continued encouragement throughout its preparation.

Preface

This book contains a translation of the court records of the trial of Elizabeth Lorentz, a young servant woman of twenty, suspected of having formed a pact with the Devil. The trial took place in the city of Brunswick, Germany, in the year 1667. We have translated the complete records, including communications with neighboring jurisdictions and advice from the nearby University of Helmstedt. Our endeavor has been to keep the translation as close to the original documents as possible, as they appear in the archival source, so that the reader can determine for herself how best to interpret the material before her. In the Appendix, we have added two documents from a second, smaller source: a description of the demonic possession of Appolonia Stampke in Brunswick in 1596, written by her pastor, Melchior Neukirch. The two documents provide a useful comparison of young women confronted with experiences of the Devil.

To illuminate these primary sources, Peter Morton has written an introductory essay that provides some cultural and historical background to the stories of Elizabeth and Appolonia. The essay focusses on one crucial aspect of the two cases out of the many that can be critically examined: both the trial of Elizabeth Lorentz and the possession of Appolonia Stampke need to be read in the context of the religious culture of early modern Germany, and specifically that of the Lutheran faith of Brunswick in the sixteenth and seventeenth centuries. Moreover, early modern Lutheran responses to human relations with the Devil themselves need to be understood against the historical developments out of which they were formed. As the Introduction examines in some detail, and as the Brunswick court itself acknowledged, it is not a simple matter to best categorize Elizabeth's relations with the Devil. We find here complex interactions between the experiences and understanding of the Devil of a young woman, and those of her community and its legal officials.

In the presentation of the primary sources, and in the introductory essay, we have tried as much as possible to leave conclusions about the two cases to the reader. There is a fundamental aspect of the trial of Elizabeth

Lorentz that the introduction does not directly address: the nature of Elizabeth's state of mind before and during the trial. This question is one that the court attempts to determine for itself, and one that we have deliberately left to the reader. The same applies to the case of Appolonia Stampke: we offer no speculation on the nature of her mental life, leaving the source document to speak for itself. The introduction provides (but hopefully is not too cluttered by) a good number of footnotes. The intent of most of these notes is to offer further readings into the different angles from which the cases can be studied. They are meant to be pointers rather than evidentiary support for any thesis of our own. We wish to note too that the Works Cited at the end of the book is not intended to be a comprehensive bibliography of the relevant fields (a project that would likely prove impossible) but exactly what it is called.

This book is closely related to another text published by the University of Toronto Press: *The Trial of Tempel Anneke: Records of a Witchcraft Trial in Brunswick, Germany, 1663* (second edition, 2017). The trials of Elizabeth Lorentz and Anna Roleffes (or Tempel Anneke) occurred in the same city within four years of one another, and many of the court officials involved in Tempel Anneke's trial appear in the records of the trial of Elizabeth Lorentz. Both trials involved suspicion of involvement with the Devil, although the verdicts reached in the two cases are different. As the introductory essay explains, there are several reasons not to see the case of Elizabeth Lorentz as a witchcraft trial, and the two cases offer some interesting contrasts.

We hope that readers of this material will find that the records offer a fascinating glimpse into the mental and cultural world of early modern Germany, and especially into the experiences of a young woman and her community.

Notes on the Translation

In our translation, we have attempted to preserve as much as possible of the original language without rendering the English too difficult to read. The reader may notice that the prose appears especially stiff and formal, an aspect of the original we have tried to replicate. Rather than attempting to convey what the original language might have sounded like to people at the time of the trial, we have kept our translation quite literal, with the intent that it sounds to a modern English-speaker the way the original sounds to a modern German-speaker. We have, however, removed irregularities in the grammar, spelling, and use of upper- and lower-case letters, to render the text readable.

We have adopted the following conventions in our translation:

- We have left Latin phrases in the original, except in the report of the physician, Laurentius Gieseler. This was done to preserve as much of the character of the original documents as possible. The Latin is often irregular and Germanized.
- We have used a single spelling for the names of people. The original documents use a variety of spellings for most names, since spelling at the time was not standardized. We have done the same for place names, using the modern spelling to make identification easier.
- The scribe uses the symbols /: ... :/ to indicate comments of his own inserted into the record of testimony. We have retained these symbols in the text, with the scribe's insertions in italics.
- Many marginal comments have been inserted into the text without indication.
- There are occasionally words that are illegible and phrases that are cut off the page, and we have indicated these with {...}.
- Our own insertions into the text, and our introductory notes, are enclosed in square brackets, as [...].

And, finally, a note on pronunciation: several words in the trial records have a vowel with an umlaut: *ä*, *ö*, or *ü*, which has the effect of placing an *e* after the vowel, as *ae*, *oe*, or *ue*. The letter *w* is always pronounced as a *v*.

Introduction: The Devil in the World of Elizabeth Lorentz

1. ELIZABETH LORENTZ AND THE DEVIL

In this book is a translation of the court records of a trial in 1667 of
Elizabeth Lorentz, a young woman of twenty, suspected of having formed
a pact with the Devil.[1] Elizabeth worked as a household servant in the
home of a brewer, Hilmar von Strombek, and his wife, Anna Geitel, in the
city of Brunswick, Germany. According to the testimony, just two weeks
after joining the household of von Strombek and Geitel, Elizabeth began
acting "melancholically," and when the family asked about the cause she
told first of having been arrested and imprisoned in the town of Sangerhausen where she had lived earlier. Before long, however, she confided to
her mistress that the Devil had come to her as a handsome well-dressed
young man, and had demanded that she kill people and have sexual intercourse with him. At first, Elizabeth was sorrowful and contrite, but when
she began to shout and threaten the family she was arrested and brought
before the court, which began an investigation into her relationship with
the Devil. To the court she confessed that during her imprisonment in
Sangerhausen she had called upon the "Evil Enemy," who later appeared
and promised to help her. Shortly after her arrival in Brunswick the Devil
came to her again, and now he said she belonged to him. During the course
of the trial she said the Devil visited her in her cell and tormented her in
the courtroom, and she told the court of terrible fear.

As a record of early modern encounters with the Devil, Elizabeth's case
is especially interesting because she does not fit easily into the common
categories of people with relationships with Satan. As this Introduction
will examine, she falls somewhere between the two most common such
relationships recognized at the time: witchcraft and demonic possession.
In the late medieval and early modern periods these two states of affairs
were most frequently associated with women. Yet Elizabeth doesn't quite

---

[1] Brunswick City Archive, B IV 15b 32.

fit either category perfectly. Diabolical witchcraft combined two crimes: the secular crime of causing harm through magic, and the spiritual crime of renouncing God and forming a pact with the Devil.[2] Elizabeth was not accused of the first of these crimes, but of the second. As she tells her story, she had called upon the Devil in a moment of distress, and since that moment he has said that she belongs to him. She denies forming an explicit pact with him, but she does say that she gave him fingernail clippings in exchange for some kernels or seeds, which the Devil instructed her to sew into her clothes to protect her from adversity. The court took this exchange as evidence of an implicit pact or agreement between them. She also claims that the Devil urged her to kill people, as he was believed to do often with witches. Significantly, Elizabeth was questioned at length whether she had had sex with the Devil, and was asked whether the Devil left a mark on her body. Both of these were common beliefs about witches. There are other elements of the trial of Elizabeth Lorentz, however, that do not readily fit trials for the crime of witchcraft. Although she is asked whether the Devil taught her magical arts, the court does not pursue the matter any further when she answers in the negative. The question appears to be standard, *pro forma*. Nor during her interrogation is she asked about participation in the witches' *sabbat*. Witches were believed to gather at the *sabbats* to worship Satan, and to take part in loathsome, blasphemous orgies. Once the concept of witchcraft became widely accepted on the European mainland, most people accused of witchcraft were questioned about attending such *sabbats*. And although she says that Satan tried to seduce her, Elizabeth claims she successfully resisted him, something not normally found among those who have confessed to a pact. Another difference that is perhaps less obvious is Elizabeth's apparent belief that she sometimes had the upper hand in her dealings with the Devil, insisting at times that she could decide what she would agree to do or refuse to do.

The possible comparison with Elizabeth's experience is demonic possession.[3] Demoniacs (people possessed by a demon) are bodily possessed: a demon enters their physical body and takes over their senses, their limbs, and their reason. Nothing like this happened to Elizabeth. She admits that the Devil tempted her and tried to seduce her into a pact, but he never possessed her bodily. What does make her case closer perhaps to possession

---

[2] For the merging of these two crimes into a single offence, see Levack (2006, pp. 32–51). The concept of witchcraft and its application to Elizabeth are explored in more detail in Section 9 below.

[3] For an introduction to the subject of demonic possession, especially in the early modern period, see Levack (2013).

Figure 1   Devil embracing a woman
Anonymous woodcut from Ulrich Molitor, *De Lamiis et Pythonicis Mulieribus*, 1489.

than to witchcraft, however, is her impression of herself as a victim of the Devil, her insistence that he tormented her and refused to leave her alone. Although she herself initiated the story that she met and conversed with the Devil, her testimony is not that of someone who entered willingly into an alliance with him, but of one who was involuntarily plagued by him. So, although it is perfectly clear that no bodily possession was involved in Elizabeth Lorentz's case, there are certain elements that are similar to cases of possession. As a supplement to the trial of Elizabeth Lorentz, therefore, we have translated a second, shorter document. This is the preface to a book of prayers published in 1596 by the pastor of the Church of St. Peter in Brunswick, Melchior Neukirch (1540–1597).[4] In his preface, Neukirch describes how Appolonia Stampke, a girl of his parish, was possessed by the Devil, and how together he and his congregation prayed and

---

[4] See Appendix of Neukirch (1596a).

worked for her release.[5] Whereas Elizabeth was suspected of voluntarily forming a pact with the Devil, Appolonia was seen by her pastor as an unwilling victim of demonic assault.

2. THE TRIAL OF ELIZABETH LORENTZ

In the seventeenth century, the region that is now Germany was part of the Holy Roman Empire, a complex of states in central Europe dating back to Charlemagne in the ninth century. The city of Brunswick was an important commercial center within the Empire, with approximately 15,000 people. It lay at the junction of important trade routes and was a member of the powerful Hanseatic League of cities, which were independent of their surrounding jurisdictions. Brunswick itself was surrounded by the duchy of Brunswick-Wolfenbüttel, in what is now the province of Lower Saxony in north-central Germany. The city had expelled the dukes in 1430, and it remained free of their rule until it was re-captured in 1671. At the time of Elizabeth's trial, the city comprised five municipalities or boroughs: Altstadt, Hagen, Neustadt, Sack, and Altewieck. Each had its own town hall, mayor and town council, court, and (except Sack) district church. There were, in addition, two independent ecclesiastical districts: the cathedral chapter of St. Blasius in the Brunswick city center, and the church and monastery of St. Aegidius in the south. For important matters of common concern there was a General Council, the *Gemeine Rat*, composed of representatives of the individual municipal councils.

Most criminal court cases were carried out under the authority of the General Council, which served as the High Court of the city.[6] Cases before the General Council were commonly presided over by a judge, called a *Syndicus*, who was trained in law. The judge was assisted by court officers: members of the General Council and senior members of one of the city guilds. In the trial of Elizabeth Lorentz, however, there was no *Syndicus* presiding over the trial. The senior officer in Elizabeth's case was Johann Schütze (or Schütte), a clothier and bedlinen maker and member of the General Council from 1662 to 1672 (Spiess 1970, p. 211). Three additional officers of the court, Joachim Gierhard, Heinrich Bahre, and Jochim Rohrbandt, are named in the record, but we can find no other mention of them. In addition to the court officers were two magistrates, Johann Velhagen and Otto Theune, full-time salaried civil servants. Velhagen was magistrate for the municipality of

---

[5] This case is discussed by Midelfort (1999, pp. 74–75). The prayers that Midelfort quotes do not appear to have been written by Appolonia, as he claims, but by Neukirch. Our thanks to Midelfort for conversation about this.

[6] Our information about the civic structure of Brunswick is largely taken from Spiess (1966).

Altstadt, and Theune was magistrate for Hagen. Finally, Johann Pilgram was the court scribe, who documented most of the testimony before the court. The trial was held in the city hall of Neustadt, the municipality where Elizabeth lived in the home of Hilmar von Strombek and Anna Geitel. The composition and setting of the court were, therefore, reflective of the unusual municipal structure of the city of Brunswick.[7]

After 1530, criminal cases within the Holy Roman Empire were conducted in accordance with an imperial criminal code, the Criminal Code of Emperor Charles V (commonly shortened to "Carolina.")[8] The Carolina stipulated the manner in which testimony was to be used before the court and outlined the stages in criminal investigation and prosecution. An important aspect of trials conducted under the Carolina was that the investigation was initiated and carried out entirely by the court. It was the court that determined whether a case should be investigated, and that identified and called witnesses to testify. We do not know the manner in which Elizabeth Lorentz was arrested, but once she was in custody the proceedings from that point were carried out under the direction and authority of the court. Trial proceedings according to the Carolina contained three distinct stages. The first stage was conducted to determine whether there was sufficient suspicion to begin formal proceedings. The Carolina recommended formal investigation into someone who is "suspected of a crime through common repute, or is notorious on account of other credible indication." During the first stage, witnesses were called but were not required to testify under oath or threat. This stage of the trial of Elizabeth Lorentz is contained in Folios 1 through 7.[9]

Once a proper criminal investigation began, witnesses and the accused testified under oath and sometimes under threat of torture. The Carolina permitted conviction for capital offences only on the grounds of confession or the testimony of two reliable eye witnesses. In the absence

---

[7] There are detailed studies of two other criminal trials in Brunswick in the late seventeenth century. Morton and Dähms (2017) contains a record of the trial of Anna Roleffes (known as Tempel Anneke) for witchcraft in 1663, and Myers (2011) is a study of the trial of Grethe Schmidt for infanticide in 1659. Myers gives a good impression of how the city of Brunswick might have appeared in the seventeenth century to poor people experiencing a large city for the first time.

[8] The complete text of the Carolina is in Schroeder (2000). For commentary see Langbein (1974) and Wiltenburg (2000). Langbein (1974, pp. 259–308) contains a translation of significant portions of the code.

[9] The Carolina does not explicitly list the spiritual crimes of heresy or demonic pact, but it does include penalties for blasphemy. See Article 106 in Schroeder (2000, p. 77). It also distinguishes between the use of sorcery to commit harm and its use with no harm done. See Article 109 in Schroeder (2000, p. 78). Only the former, it says, should be punished with death.

of such witnesses the court was directed to proceed to torture to seek a confession.[10] The second stage of a trial was therefore intended to determine whether there was what the Carolina called "legally sufficient indication" to proceed to torture. The largest part of the Carolina was devoted to outlining the circumstances that constitute such indication for crimes of various sorts. The second part of the trial of Elizabeth Lorentz is recorded in Folios 8 through 14. Since some of her testimony concerned her imprisonment in the town of Sangerhausen, the court wrote to officials there asking for complete information about her trial in that town. That letter and the reply from Sangerhausen constitute Folios 8 and 9. Included with the letter from Sangerhausen was a copy of the judgment reached there, and in that judgment the court determined that Elizabeth was "not of full reason by all accounts, but rather brought forward what she reported out of sadness and despair." The Brunswick court therefore brought in a physician to investigate Elizabeth's mental condition. This person was Laurentius Gieseler, the *Stadtphysicus*, who we would now describe as chief medical officer of the city. Like the *Syndici*, the *Stadtphysicus* was among the highest and best-paid officers of the city, appointed directly by the General Council. Gieseler's report to the court is contained in Folio 11. Folios 12 and 13 of the records document the lengthy formal interrogation of Elizabeth, concentrating in detail on her alleged relations with the Devil. Folio 14 documents a very peculiar and interesting episode in the trial, apparently initiated by Elizabeth herself, in which they investigate a bailiff for his conduct towards the imprisoned.

A central stipulation for trials conducted in accordance with the Carolina was that the records of the proceedings be forwarded to the legal faculty of a university to receive its advice before moving to the third stage, the application of torture. Such a report was called a *Gutachten*, and it was a major function of university legal faculties to review criminal cases and provide such advice. This requirement was put in place by the Empire because many jurisdictions did not have officers trained in law, and both legal decisions and the use of torture varied widely. A fundamental goal of the Carolina, therefore, was to bring about informed and uniform judgments. The Brunswick court obtained a *Gutachten* for the trial of Elizabeth Lorentz from the University of Helmstedt, which constitutes Folio 15. In that document, the

---

[10] Although torture was not used in the trial of Elizabeth Lorentz, it is important to note for general purposes that torture was not intended to produce conviction of an innocent person, and safeguards were included in the instructions to ensure that it was used only to obtain information that could not be acquired in other ways. If the accused did not confess under torture, he or she was to be released. In practice, however, these safeguards could be ignored, as happened in the worst of the witchcraft trials. See Levack (2006, pp. 80–88).

Figure 2 Sundial outside the church in Gorsleben, where
Elizabeth Lorentz lived before she moved to Brunswick.
Extremam reputa quamlibet esse tibi
"Consider that each [hour] could be your last."

university academics determine that, while on the one hand it appeared that Elizabeth did enter into an implicit pact with the Devil, she was nonetheless to be taken as a person "strongly plagued" by the Evil Enemy, and so no torture was to be used against her. Rather she was to be put into the care of "pious and God-fearing people." Based on the advice of the university, the court ordered that Elizabeth be released, but she was banished from the city forever.

3. A WORLD DISORDERED

The people of the times in which Elizabeth Lorentz and Appolonia Stampke lived experienced a fear of the Devil that was greater and more influential than that of both earlier and later times. But this fear did not originate during this period; its history traces at least to the late Middle Ages, between 1350 and 1500. It is important, first, to note the degree to which religious ritual shaped the worldview of Christian society in Western Europe at that time.[11] Throughout the medieval period, Christian liturgy assumed increasing significance in the seasonal cycle of social activity. The rites of the medieval church provided a religious framework for social cohesion, and communal participation in the mass created a social structure within which the members of the community were bound both as individuals and as a single unity by relations that were part of a sacred order.[12] Religious ritual was also important to the sense of security and trust in the cosmic order. Both the "official" rituals of the church—the sacraments, the mass, and the annual cycle of feast days—and the less official rituals of sacred processions, blessings, and popular devotions created a sense that human activity contributed to the maintenance of a universal order upon which life depended.[13] Thus, "rituals created orderly relationships with the sacred powers on which the world and human life depended, as well as among humans and between humans and the material world. When any kind of disorder threatened this world, people were able to use various rites and rituals to overcome that disorder" (Scribner 1988, p. 125).

Within this context, Western Europe in the late Middle Ages experienced a form of spiritual crisis.[14] First, from the middle of the fourteenth

---

[11] The distinction between Eastern and Western Europe at the time can be drawn on the basis of the two Christian churches: the Orthodox Church, based in Constantinople, and the Catholic Church, based in Rome.

[12] This theme was especially developed by John Bossy (1983 and 1985). See Reinburg (1992) on the participation of the laity in the late medieval mass. See also Biller (1997) and the essays on confession and penance in Biller and Minnis (1998).

[13] On this, see especially Scribner (1987b). For collections of his work, see Scribner (1987a) and (2011).

[14] For statements of this view, see Lindberg (2010, pp. 23–53) and Oberman (1973, pp. 16–20).

century, the region experienced a succession of socio-economic crises of agricultural production and wealth distribution, which resulted in widespread famines and social uprisings. Much more devastating, however, was the horrific Black Death, which swept across Europe beginning in the mid-fourteenth century, depopulating entire regions. In response to the plague, devout Christians turned increasingly to an affective piety, with a heightened emotionalism and concentration on the suffering and death of Christ.[15] Third, the Roman Catholic Church, which was, at that time, the only church in Western Europe, faced its own succession of difficulties, both within the hierarchy of the church itself and within the wider Christian community: the so-called papal schisms of the fourteenth century, in which competing popes excommunicated one another; a growing awareness of inadequacies and corruption among the clergy; and an ongoing struggle for leadership between the popes in Rome and the councils of bishops. In addition, there had been repeated attempts to reform the doctrines of the church and return it to what was perceived to be its original purity. There were groups that sought a form of Christianity outside the official church, who were declared heretical and fiercely persecuted by the Inquisition. These were represented most clearly by the sects known as Cathars and Waldensians. Protest also occurred within the church. In England, the priest and Oxford theologian John Wycliffe (c. 1330–1384) attacked the established doctrines and practices of the church, calling for radical reform. The Bohemian Jan Hus (1369–1415) drew on Wycliffe's writings, and, following Hus's execution, his followers rose up in open revolt.

In a society that perceived the structure and harmony of the world to reside in the sacred, these spiritual, social, and natural crises indicated a world in disarray. The political and spiritual struggles of the late medieval church gave an appearance of disorder within the institution at the center of religious life. The successions of wars, plagues, and social uprisings in a world thought to be ordered by sacred powers further contributed to this sense of imbalance and disarray. From all of this emerged a growing belief in God's anger and disappointment with his people, a sense among the devout that human beings had offended God, whose wrath was witnessed in the disordered world. From the early fifteenth century onward, fear of the Devil also began to increase among those attempting to reform the church. In earlier representations, the primary role of the Devil is one of temptation, of luring people away from God, as he did with Adam and

---

[15] For the effect of the Black Death on forms of spirituality, see Jost (2016a) and (2016b), and Cantor (2001).

Eve. In this role, he is an enemy of Christ, whose purpose is to draw people towards God. But in the later Middle Ages, the Devil began to appear as an enemy of God, a figure of evil standing in opposition to God and his creation (Bossy 1988, p. 229). It was at this time that Christian authorities, especially members of the Dominican order, forged the concept of diabolical witchcraft, according to which legions of witches brought about sickness, death, and destruction through formal pacts with the Devil.[16]

The spiritual crises of the late Middle Ages coincided with an increased emphasis on sin in the moral discipline of the church, generated by demand for regular confession before a priest, beginning in the thirteenth century, and the gradual replacement of the seven deadly sins by the Ten Commandments as the basis for moral instruction.[17] Steven Ozment (1975, pp. 15–46) argues that the emphasis on sin and penance in late medieval confessional manuals created an endless regime of self-examination.[18] Demand for internalized reflection on sin combined with the outward displays of piety reflected in the many rituals, observances, and popular devotions that punctuated daily life. Devout Christians of the late Middle Ages, therefore, faced the question: What is necessary in order to earn God's forgiveness, both for oneself and for loved ones?

4. MARTIN LUTHER AND THE PROTESTANT REFORMATION

The events just described occurred in the centuries before the documents translated in this book, and so they constitute only a broad historical background against which we can place the period of Elizabeth's and Appolonia's experiences. In the sixteenth century, a further development occurred that was profoundly important to the communities of these two young women: the Protestant Reformation.[19] Before this event, there was only one church in Western Europe, the Catholic Church, centered in Rome and led by the pope. The year most often associated with the beginning of the Reformation is 1517. It was on October 31 of that year that the monk, priest, and professor at the University of Wittenberg, Martin Luther (1483–1546), made public his so-called Ninety-Five Theses, which were harshly critical

---

[16] It is important to note that, although the idea of witchcraft was initially formed by church authorities, after 1500, in the northern regions of Europe, trials of those accused of witchcraft were conducted exclusively by secular courts.

[17] See Slattery (1979), Bossy (1988), and Bast (1997, pp. 1–45). For a criticism of Bossy's conclusions, see Morton (2018).

[18] For a criticism of Ozment's assessment of late medieval pastoral care, see Tentler (1977) and Duggan (1984).

[19] Three reliable general guides to the Reformation from different points of view are Ozment (1980), Lindberg (2010), and McGrath (2012).

of certain aspects of the Catholic Church. Luther's criticisms of the church came out of the long period of crisis that was sketched in the previous section, and many of his demands reflected those of John Wycliffe and Jan Hus before him. Yet unlike these earlier events, which the church managed to contain, control, or suppress, Martin Luther's confrontations with the ecclesiastical authorities that followed his action of 1517 split the Western church apart.

In his early years, Luther shared the late medieval sense of spiritual crisis sketched in Section 3. He was born at the end of the fifteenth century, and his beliefs were formed against the backdrop of spiritual anguish and fear of God's wrath that so influenced life in the late Middle Ages. When he was a young monk of the Augustinian order, this anguish took the form of despair over losing or failing to obtain the love and forgiveness of God, and as a result he struggled desperately to lead a life worthy of God's grace. But at a certain point somewhere between 1513 and 1515 the depth of Luther's anguish led to a personal and theological breakthrough. In this breakthrough, he came to reject the very idea that human beings could earn God's love and forgiveness through penance.[20] Upon re-reading St. Paul's *Epistle to the Romans*, Luther arrived at a radically new conception of righteousness. According to his new thinking, righteousness is not a property that human beings can acquire by means of striving in this world. It is rather something that God bestows upon his undeserving people through his divine mercy and the sacrifice of Jesus Christ alone.[21] Christ, then, is not a harsh judge who comes to assess our righteousness before God, but one who through his death brought mercy and forgiveness to the undeserving. We cannot therefore earn God's love through penance or good works, for we are hopelessly mired in sin, but we can receive that love, despite our sin, through faith. Faith does not earn God's mercy, but opens the door to it. As a response to the anguish that he had inherited from his religious background, this thought was for Luther a profoundly liberating revelation.

There was another facet of Luther's thought that we should recognize, which he inherited from certain late medieval theologians. This was his belief that we cannot form an understanding of God's relationship to human beings through the use of our natural reason.[22] In Luther's opinion,

---

[20] Two useful guides to Luther's theology are Althaus (1966) and Lohse (2011). Luther's writings in English are collected in Luther (1955–2016).

[21] See McGrath (2012, pp. 115–27).

[22] Luther believed that without revelation human beings could know of the existence of a divine creator and understand the rules of moral conduct. This much the pagan Greeks and Romans had managed. But humans needed the revelation provided by Scripture in order to have any knowledge of divine grace and providence.

God's mercy is not something we can rationally explain, or form an understanding of through a reasoned study of the natural order. It is shown to us solely in the person of Jesus Christ and his sacrifice on the cross. God made himself human in order to reveal his mercy, and this fact is knowable only through Scripture. Moreover, we cannot know what form God's mercy will take, since its origin and nature are beyond our reach. This applies in particular to our experiences of suffering. When we are beset by pain and suffering we must believe that God himself has chosen this for us through his deep love, even though his reasons are not apparent. As told in the biblical stories of Job and Lazarus, even when we have lost everything and suffer the worst torments, we must not abandon our faith in God's wisdom and mercy. This aspect of Luther's theology had profound implications for the best Christian response to the Devil: in his wisdom, God has chosen the suffering and temptations brought upon us by Satan, and it is only through our Christian faith that we can withstand them. According to Lutheran doctrine, no purely human act can bring about anything not chosen by God, and this includes protection from the Devil. This assertion stood against centuries of both sanctioned and unsanctioned Christian ritual defenses against the Devil, which had formed a part of both medieval church practice and central elements of popular culture.

5. THE PROTESTANT REFORMATION
IN BRUNSWICK

Luther's defiance of the church authorities spread rapidly across the regions of Europe north of the Alps and east of the Pyrenees. Those who followed Luther in rejecting central doctrines of the Catholic Church are referred to now as Protestants. To Luther's dismay, however, Protestants could not agree on what to replace Catholic doctrine with. Major disputes broke out over a number of central theological issues.[23] By the middle of the sixteenth century it was no longer possible to speak of *the* Christian church in the West, but only of many churches. Within the Holy Roman Empire, two churches predominated: the Roman Catholic and the Lutheran. Between 1540 and 1648 these two were in fierce competition, and at times, through the princes of their respective territories, in open warfare. After an outbreak of warfare in 1546, the princes of the Empire agreed in 1555 on the principal *Cuius regio, eius religio* ("Whose realm, his religion"), which stated that the ruler of each state would determine the religion of its subjects, and limited the forms of religion to Catholic and Lutheran.

---

[23] See McGrath (2012, pp. 163–90 and 191–206), and for disputes among Lutherans, see Dingel (2008).

This division eventually contributed to the massively destructive Thirty Years War between 1618 and 1648.

The Reformation came early to the city of Brunswick, when the city and its churches adopted the doctrines and practices of Martin Luther in the years immediately following his break from the Catholic Church. Writings of Luther's were published by Brunswick's first printer as early as 1518.[24] In 1521 and 1522, a Benedictine monk, Gottschalk Kruse (c. 1499–1540) of the St. Aegidius monastery in Brunswick, preached according to Luther's teachings, which he had learned from the reformer himself in Wittenberg. Kruse was twice forced to flee the city after charges of teaching heresy, but he nonetheless published two defenses of Lutheran doctrines in Brunswick, which seemingly ignited great interest within the city.[25] By 1527, popular Reformation preachers had abolished the Catholic mass in the Church of St. Martin. Most importantly, in 1528, the Wittenberg reformer Johannes Bugenhagen (1485–1558) published the Brunswick Church Ordinance, which was officially adopted by the city council for all its churches.[26] Brunswick's importance for the Lutheran Church was further solidified by the appointment of two theologians from Wittenberg, Joachim Mörlin (1514–1571) and Martin Chemnitz (1522–1586), as joint church superintendents between 1553 and 1567. Between them, these two reformers struggled to resolve a number of controversies that arose between the followers of Martin Luther after Luther's death in 1546. The result of their work was the Corpus Doctrinae Prutenicum (The Prussian Body of Doctrine), printed in 1567.[27] Ten years later, this document formed the basis of a crucial text, The Formula of Concord, which was put forward as the authoritative statement of the Lutheran faith.[28] Between Bugenhagen's church ordinance and the efforts of the two Brunswick theologians, the city thus was at the center of the establishment of the Lutheran Church in the formative years of the sixteenth century.

---

[24] See Luther (1518).

[25] Gottschalk Kruse (1522) and (1523). Kruse went on to advance the Reformation in nearby jurisdictions before being called by Duke Ernst of Brunswick-Lüneburg to serve as pastor and prefect of the Lutheran Church in the ducal residence city of Celle.

[26] Bugenhagen (1912). Thereafter Bugenhagen wrote church ordinances based on the Brunswick model in cities across northern Germany and Denmark and played a leading role in their implementation. For this he was referred to as the Apostle of the Reformation. See Lindberg (2010, pp. 118–29).

[27] Kolb (2004) gives a good overview of this work and its significance for the Lutheran Church.

[28] See Kolb and Wengert (2000, pp. 481–523). In 1563, Mörlin and Chemnitz published Bugenhagen's church ordinance together with a collection of declarations and defenses of Lutheran doctrine, called the Braunschweiger Corpus Doctrinae, modelled on Philip Melanchthon's book of the same name. These kinds of documents, produced in various cities, provided models for the Book of Concord of 1580, which was widely accepted as the doctrinal canon of the Lutheran Church. An English translation of the latter is Kolb and Wengert (2000).

While Brunswick joined the Lutheran Church early, the surrounding duchy of Brunswick-Wolfenbüttel did not adopt Lutheranism until 1568, with the ascendency of Duke Julius (1528–1589). Julius signed the Formula of Concord in 1577, and he also founded a Lutheran university in nearby Helmstedt, the *Academia Julia*, which attracted a number of influential scientists, physicians, and theologians. Under Julius's successor, Heinrich Julius (1564–1613), a variety of Christian humanism flourished at the university: a science and theology cultivated by Luther's colleague, Philip Melanchthon, that combined Scriptural reading with the study of classical languages and literature. Its adherents, in Helmstedt and elsewhere, were opposed to the emphasis on doctrinal purity found among the so-called orthodox Lutherans, of whom Joachim Mörlin had been a strong representative. The church superintendents of Brunswick, however, resisted the humanistic trend in Helmstedt until 1646, partly out of resistance among the burgher class to influence from the duchy.

Another religious influence that conflicted with Lutheran orthodoxy in Brunswick was Pietism, a movement founded in the mid-century at the University of Halle by Philipp Spener (1635–1705). Pietists shared with traditional Lutherans a belief in the foundation of faith in Scripture, but they emphasized inner spirituality over theological doctrine. Although Lutheran Pietism did not become well established until late in the seventeenth century, its influence may have been felt in Brunswick around the time of Elizabeth's trial.[29] Thus, while Brunswick remained loyal until the middle of the seventeenth century to the orthodox doctrines established by Mörlin and Chemnitz, there were continuous pressures from movements that were opposed to the strong adherence to doctrine as defining Christian life. It is within this specific religious context that we need to study the events involving Appolonia Stampke and Elizabeth Lorentz.

6. ELIZABETH'S PLACE IN A LUTHERAN URBAN HOUSEHOLD

Like most common people who came before the courts in early modern Europe, we know nothing about Elizabeth Lorentz beyond what is contained in the trial records. But the information contained there can be placed into the context of what we know about German society at the

---

[29] One of the anonymous reviewers of this text suggested that the rise of Pietism might have had an influence on Elizabeth. In the 1690s there were several cases of suspected demonic possession among "ecstatic" Pietist girls and women in north Germany. See Stitziel (1996) and Midelfort (2016). On Pietism generally, see Shantz (2013 and 2015).

time.[30] Her father, Andreas Lorentz, was a soldier in Brunswick until six years before her trial. Elizabeth mentions that he had been in service for twenty-four years and had a regular post, and it is likely that she added this detail to indicate that he was a respectable citizen.[31] Her mother's name was Anna Triebel. After Andreas's discharge the family moved to the town of Sangerhausen, on the far side of the Harz Mountains to the southeast, where she says her father worked as a blacksmith.[32] With Andreas's death a year later, Anna Triebel would have found herself without economic security, for means of income for women outside of the household had been shrinking since the Middle Ages. She seems to have scraped a living from lace work and odd jobs. Although apprenticeships for girls were possible, for example, in midwifery, it would have been assumed that Elizabeth would seek security in a marriage. Her mother would not have been able to provide her daughters with a dowry, and so Elizabeth was put into domestic service. This was normal practice, and the chores of maid-servants often served informally as an apprenticeship to the responsibilities of a wife (Read 2015, p. 17).

Just a few months before the trial, Elizabeth moved back to Brunswick and entered service in the household of a brewer, Hilmar von Strombek, and his wife, Anna Geitel. The word "household" is key to understanding the domestic world that Elizabeth entered. The early modern German urban household was far more than the house of a single family. It constituted the core of economic, social, and moral life of the city. Since the Middle Ages, economic affairs in German cities had been dominated by the craft and merchant guilds: commercial collectives that licensed and regulated the activity of each trade. The members of the guilds were masters of their trade, licensed by their guild to practice and to train apprentices. The household of the master was the site of his business and workshop as well as the home of his family; under the roof of the house lived the master and mistress, their children, servants, and apprentices. Von Strombek himself would have been a relatively well-to-do member of the burgher class in the city, having more than one servant and employing his own brew-master. Families in Brunswick with a license to brew beer were proud families, marching at the head of the city procession at Corpus Christi (Spiess 1966, p. 231). Moreover, most brew-masters in

---

[30] For introductions to the daily lives of women in early modern Europe, see Wiesner (1993), Read (2015), and the essays in Raber (2013).

[31] Many soldiers of the time were mercenaries, and in the decades after the Thirty Years War they had a reputation for unruly and violent behavior.

[32] In their communication with the Brunswick court (Folio 9), however, the court in Sangerhausen says he was a farmer in the village of Gorsleben.

Brunswick were itinerant, moving from one family to another, so the fact that von Strombek employed his own speaks to his stature. Elizabeth entered a household of a well-established burgher family.

In the fourteenth and fifteenth centuries, the middle classes of Brunswick struggled with the patrician families of the city to establish a place on the city council, and disparities in wealth and power among the trades also led to several uprisings and riots. By the time the Reformation came to Brunswick, members of the leading craft guilds had established positions on the city council, and their values and interests were influential.[33] The power of the burgher class in German cities both reinforced and fundamentally altered the impact of the Reformation. In the 1520s, Luther's exhortation to throw off the religious authority of the Roman Church, together with his message of righteousness through faith, promoted a sense of both civic and religious freedom among his followers in Germany.[34] Ultimately, however, within Protestant German cities like Brunswick, city councils became the moral authorities of their society.[35] It was the city council that invited Johannes Bugenhagen to Brunswick and that appointed Joachim Mörlin and Martin Chemnitz as church superintendents; the decisions to adopt church ordinances and declarations of religious doctrine lay also with the council. Another way in which civic leaders implemented their moral authority was through civic ordinances, which contained declarations of religious doctrine, codes of law and punishment, and exhortations to modest and pious behavior. In 1579, Brunswick adopted a comprehensive civic ordinance, covering religious faith, criminal law, civil discipline, and governance.[36] In the same year the city issued a further ordinance governing clothing, bodily adornment, engagement and marriage, the purpose of which was to enforce frugality, modesty, and respect for one's station in society.[37]

---

[33] We have found no mention of von Strombek himself on the city council, however.

[34] Ozment (1975, pp. 47–120) describes the sense of emancipation the Reformation inspired. The spirit of the early years of the movement can be seen in the writings of Katharina Schütz Zell (1497–1562). See Zell (2006).

[35] This was a complex development over a long period of time. The alliances formed between the leaders of the Reformation, the territorial princes, and city councils of the Holy Roman Empire are a central subject in histories of the Reformation.

[36] *Der Stadt Braunschweig Ordnung* (2002).

[37] *Die Berühmte Braunschweiger Stadt und Kleider Ordnung* (1978). For example, regarding the clothing of maid-servants, the ordinance says, "Maidservants here shall wear no better bodice than cloth, and no finer silk band than of fourteen Mariengroschen worth. The fine shall be one New Shilling for each time a maid transgresses this our proscription" (p. 10r). Clothing thus served to reinforce and make visible the distinctions between classes and roles in society.

A subject of considerable discussion among historians has been the impact that the Reformation had on women's lives, especially within the context of marriage and the household.[38] In promoting clerical marriage in place of celibacy, Protestants argued that the marital relationship is a divine creation grounded in Scripture, thereby enshrining marriage as the basis of godly society.[39] Further, the commandment to "love the Lord your God with all your heart and with all your soul and with all your mind" (Matthew 22:35–40),[40] on which Protestants placed special emphasis, could be applied to patriarchal framework in which father, civic authority, and church stand in a hierarchical order under God.[41] In his book *When Fathers Ruled* (1983), Steven Ozment emphasizes the positive ideals of marriage represented in Reformation pamphlet literature and handbooks, in contrast to the Catholic ideal of celibacy and the institutional rigidity of medieval marriage. In contrast, in her 1991 study of Augsburg, *The Holy Household*, Lyndal Roper argues that, despite the early Reformation messages of freedom and the positive view the Reformers held of marriage, the adoption of patriarchal morality into the Reformation weakened the position of women in the household. In a study of Lutheran printed literature of the sixteenth century, Marjorie Elizabeth Plummer (1996) argues that while reformers prided themselves on having a more positive image of women than that of their Catholic rivals, they believed that only within the context of a marriage could a woman fulfill her proper role and protect herself from sin. Susan C. Karant-Nunn (1997) argues that church and state together used the opportunity to restructure the rituals surrounding birth, baptism, marriage, and death to impose the moral discipline needed for a Christian society.[42] More recently, Kathleen Crowther (publishing as Crowther-Heyck 2002, 2003; publishing as Crowther 2010) closely examines ways in which Reformation religious discourse, and especially the descriptions of Creation and the Fall, shaped understandings of marital relations, conception, pregnancy, and childbirth.

7. RELIGIOUS INSTRUCTION

The moral order just described was reinforced through education and religious instruction, to which both Appolonia Stampke and Elizabeth Lorentz were exposed. We can identify one of the key sources of Elizabeth's

---

[38] The literature on this subject is large, and what is offered here is only a sampling. For a useful overview, see Wiesner-Hanks (2006).
[39] See Plummer (1996, pp. 30–100).
[40] New International Version.
[41] On this subject, see Bast (1997).
[42] See also Karant-Nunn (1998).

instruction from her answer to Question 7 of Folio 7 in the trial records. She is asked by the court whether she knows the Second Commandment, and she immediately answers, "You should not take the name of God the Lord in vain. Because the Lord will not leave the one who misuses his name unpunished," which she says means, "we are supposed to fear and love God, so that with his name we don't curse, do magic, lie or cheat, but call to him in all adversity, pray to him, praise, and thank him." These words are an exact quotation from *The Small Catechism*, a book by Martin Luther that outlines the central elements of Christian faith in a form that is easily remembered and recited.[43] Elizabeth may have learned this work as preparation for her first communion (Christman 2008, pp. 273–74). She also says that her parents put her in school to learn to read and write, and it is quite possible that she learned by copying and reading aloud from *The Small Catechism*.[44]

The Small Catechism was at the core of a program of religious instruction undertaken by Luther and his followers.[45] From as early as 1525 reformers in Wittenberg had begun work on a book of instruction in the faith. Their perception of the need for such a work was strengthened when parish inspections carried out in Saxony in 1526 to 1528 revealed a very poor knowledge of Christian doctrine among the parishioners and the pastors alike.[46] In part, this was because piety among the ordinary people prior to the Reformation had not been manifested through learning of texts and knowledge of doctrine, but through experiential elements of ritual and practice.[47] To amend this situation, in 1529 Luther published two educational texts: the Large and Small Catechisms.[48] The former was intended for those charged with preaching and education, and the latter,

---

[43] The term "catechism" is from the Greek for oral instruction and in early Christendom referred to preparation for baptism. With the adoption of infant baptism, the word came to denote instruction for children in preparation for communion.

[44] The establishment of schools for children was an important component in the Protestant Reformation movements. One historian estimates that by 1618, in most territories, every Lutheran congregation had a school for boys, and schools that taught reading, writing, and the catechisms for girls were introduced over the seventeenth century. See Christman (2008, p. 276).

[45] In this they were continuing a late medieval program of catechesis, especially associated with the French theologian and educator Jean Gerson, Chancellor of the University of Paris from 1395.

[46] In his Preface to *The Small Catechism*, Luther writes, "Dear God, what misery I beheld! The ordinary person, especially in the villages, knows absolutely nothing of the Christian faith, and unfortunately many pastors are completely unskilled and incompetent teachers" (Kolb and Wengert 2000, p. 347).

[47] There had been efforts since the early thirteenth century, however, to teach the elements of the faith to ordinary people in preparation for confession.

[48] See Kolb and Wengert (2000, pp. 345–480).

written in a question-and-answer form derived from medieval catechisms, was intended for ordinary people. The first three parts of *The Small Catechism* contain instruction in fundamental statements of faith: the Ten Commandments, the Apostle's Creed, and the Lord's Prayer. The order of these parts of the catechism reflects the idea that from the law (the Commandments) we learn of our sins and from the gospel of Christ we learn of God's forgiveness. To these Luther added sections on baptism, confession, and communion. As Lee Palmer Wandel (2015, pp. 15–16) says, the intent of these two texts was that they would encapsulate in words what it means to be a Christian.[49] By the seventeenth century, *The Small Catechism* had "become canonized as *the* textual basis for all religious instruction in many Lutheran areas" (Bode 2008, p. 180).[50] Its many editions were often supplemented with additional questions and answers, hymns, and prayers.

One of the central messages in the catechisms, which was widely reflected in Lutheran literature and sermons, was the importance of every member of the household fulfilling their proper role well.[51] For example, in the section on confession in *The Small Catechism*, to the question: "Which sins should a person confess?" Luther says, "Here reflect on your walk of life in light of the Ten Commandments: Whether you are father, mother, son, daughter, master, mistress, servant." And he gives as an example a confession for a servant as follows:

I, a poor sinner, confess before God that I am guilty of all my sins. In particular I confess in your presence that although I am a manservant or maidservant, etc., I unfortunately serve my master unfaithfully, for in this and that instance I did not do what they told me; I made them angry and caused them to curse; I neglected to do my duty, and allowed harm to occur. I have also been immodest in word and deed. I have quarreled with my equals. I have grumbled and sworn at my mistress, etc. For all this I am sorry and pray for grace. I want to do better. (Dingel 2014, p. 886)[52]

Elizabeth would thus have learned that faithfully serving her master and carrying out her duties in the household were duties she owed primarily to God. Reciprocally, the head of the household—the *Hausvater*—was responsible for teaching his children and servants. In the confession for

---

[49] See Wandel's (2015) work for an analysis of the major catechisms of the early modern period.

[50] This work, and Christman (2008) in the same volume, give good overviews of instruction in the catechism. Strauss (1978) remains a good study of Lutheran teaching. Strauss's negative assessment of the success of the program generated great controversy.

[51] This is documented by Plummer (1996).

[52] Our translation is based on Kolb and Wengert (2000, p. 360) and Tappert (1959, p. 350).

masters, the text says, "I confess in your presence that I have not been faithful in training my children, servants, and wife to the glory of God. I have cursed. I have set a bad example by my immodest language and actions" (Dingel 2014, p. 886). Lutherans emphasized that, while a good *Hausvater* would bring a household together, a wild, reckless husband could destroy it (Plummer 1996, p. 204).[53] Von Strombek and his wife, Anna Geitel, would therefore likely have felt some Christian responsibility for Elizabeth, although she was not in their service for very long.

Another source of Elizabeth's religious influences would have been sermons she heard in church.[54] Despite the impact of printing, early modern culture was still predominantly oral, and Lutherans placed considerable emphasis on hearing the Word of God. Ironically perhaps, the importance of the sermon to the Lutheran Church is witnessed by the astonishing number of printed sermons that poured off the presses in the sixteenth century. The foundation of Lutheran preaching was always the Bible, either by framing the message of the sermon around a specific passage of Scripture, or by supporting it with large numbers of biblical citations. A degree of uniformity in message was provided by postils: collections of sermons intended for the use of pastors in preparing their own.[55] A very large such collection was written over many years by Joachim Mörlin.[56] Each sermon is prefaced by a passage from the Bible, which is followed by an explanation of the message to be drawn from it. The themes were often ones of repentance, divine forgiveness of sins, and trust in God. For example, early modern Lutheran preaching on the sacrifice of Christ on the cross presented his suffering as atonement for our sins, and hence as a source of comfort and strength. In Mörlin's postil for the Thursday of Passion Week he writes,

And who would be horrified of dying or of some misery? While we carry the guarantee of our salvation in our poor blood and flesh at all times. So indeed, this is what it is about: that in his Sacrament he lets us know that he wants to be with us and beside us in all need, until we are in the hereafter, where he sits in the eternal kingdom of his father. If the

---

[53] Plummer (1996, p. 187) notes, however, that the duties of husbands in the spiritual training of the household, as described in sixteenth-century Lutheran literature, were reduced in the late sixteenth and early seventeenth centuries.

[54] A useful survey of Lutheran preaching is Haeming and Kolb (2008).

[55] Karant-Nunn (1997, p. 126) argues that these postils rendered sermons "tediously similar," a view not supported by Haeming and Kolb (2008, p. 127).

[56] See Mörlin (1587).

Devil or the world tears our head off, what has he gained? Or what have we lost? (Mörlin 1587, p. 305)

With these kinds of exposures, Elizabeth would have understood the Lutheran faith through the lens of a carefully constructed program of instruction. This would have included her understanding of the Devil and his action in the world. We need, then, to understand something of how Lutherans understood the nature and role of the Devil.

8. THE DEVIL AND THE CONCEPT OF *ANFECHTUNG*

Martin Luther was born into a Christian social world in which belief in the reality of the Devil was universal. For Luther, too, the Devil was an immensely frightening being, but he understood this in a particular way as a consequence of his new conception of righteousness. Given his fundamental idea that righteousness is an undeserved gift of God, Luther interpreted sin as an attempt by human beings to establish their own righteousness before God (Lohse 2011, p. 71). We sin when we see our own interests and our own virtues as superior to those given to us by God. Human nature, according to Luther, "knows nothing but its own good, or what is good and honorable and useful for itself, but not what is good for God and other people" (Luther 1955–2016, Volume 25, p. 345).[57] The Devil is the complete embodiment of this revolt against God, attempting to set himself up against God and wanting to bring humankind into his revolt with him. At the same time, however, Luther argued that the Devil is nonetheless a creation of God, and as such he is infinitely less powerful than God in every way. The Devil exists within the divine order, not to destroy people, but to bring Christians to God. For it is through the temptations and torments of the Devil, Luther argued, that we begin to despair of our ability to earn God's love. In one of his Table Talks, recorded by his friends, Luther says,

It's the Devil who makes people think this way, saying, "Ah, you must believe this. You must believe more. Your faith is not very strong and it's still not enough." In this way, he compels them to despair. We are so constituted that by nature we desire to have a conscious faith. We'd like to grab it with our hands and shove it into our heart, but this doesn't happen in our earthly life. We can't comprehend it, but we ought to

---

[57] Quoted in Lohse (2011, p. 71).

apprehend it. We should thus hold on to the Word and let it drag us along. (Quoted in Eire 2005, p. 82)[58]

Luther argued that it is only when we realize the hopelessness of earning salvation, given the sinful character of human nature and the immense strength of the Devil, that we can come to realize that our only possible salvation lies with God. In this way, then, it is paradoxically through the Devil that human beings can come to God. Without this realization, we will continue to seek righteousness in our own image. Thus, the Devil is simultaneously the worst evil that Christians can confront, drawing us into open rebellion against God, and yet also the source of the ultimate despair that can finally lead us to proper faith in God's mercy and free us of the Devil entirely.

At the core of Luther's understanding of the relationship between Christians and the Devil was the concept of what he called *Anfechtung* (*Anfechtungen* is the plural form). The term occurs frequently in the trial of Elizabeth Lorentz, describing the attacks on her by the Devil. Today it is usually translated as "temptation," but more precisely it refers to temptation in the form of spiritual assault. The connection between *Anfechtung* and the Devil gives us a framework within which to analyze the experiences of Elizabeth Lorentz. The officials of the court use the term when they question her about her mental state and about her dealings with the Devil. In our translation of the trial records we have left the term in the original German, because its meaning is complex and cannot be captured by any one English term. This word, *Anfechtung*, is also the source of the title of this book. In cataloguing the records of Elizabeth's trial, some archivist or other wrote on the cover page, "*Elizabeth Lorentz: Wegen Anfechtung des Teufels.*" This would normally be translated as "Elizabeth Lorentz: Concerning Temptation by the Devil." But for the title of our book we have used a loose translation, "The Bedevilment of Elizabeth Lorentz," which perhaps conveys something closer to what the situation involved. The term *Anfechtung* is also used by Melchior Neukirch in his descriptions of the possession of Appolonia Stampke to describe the attacks on her by the Devil. The concept was therefore central to the understandings of demonic involvement that shaped the cases of Elizabeth and Appolonia.

The word was especially important to Martin Luther himself, and he understood its meaning in terms of his own spiritual struggle and his

---

[58] The article by Eire (2005) is useful as a study of Luther's understanding of a Christian's relationship with the Devil, especially in Luther's later years.

ultimate revelation of righteousness as an undeserved gift of God.[59] First, for him the term denoted his despair in the face of his own sins and the terrifying judgment of God. In this sense, *Anfechtung* was for Luther a negative source of fear and lack of faith. Yet it was through this despair that he was ultimately led to the revelation that his salvation was completely out of his hands and rested only with God, and was thus led to his solution of righteousness as divine gift. In this realization Luther stressed the positive role of *Anfechtung* in leading Christians to recognize God's mercy. While *Anfechtung* can lead to despair and helplessness, it is precisely through this despair that it leads to faith. Moreover, Luther also believed that suffering was an essential aspect of Christian life, for without reminders of our weaknesses we easily forget our dependence upon God and assume that our comfort is achieved through our own efforts alone. Thus, the misfortunes that befall us—the death of a child, the loss of crops through storms—were for Luther the means by which ordinary Christians come to realize that both temporal relief and eternal salvation are possible only through the merciful intervention of Christ.[60] These everyday misfortunes too were forms of *Anfechtung*. In his own personal struggle, then, the notion of *Anfechtung* conveyed for Luther the tribulations that first created his despair, but ultimately led him to faith and then preserved it.

Given the role of the Devil in the divine order as the one who drives us away from God and into despair, he was seen by Luther as the primary source of *Anfechtungen* in Christian life. In his initial act of tempting Adam and Eve into rebellion, Satan brought sin and suffering into the world. According to the theology that Luther inherited from St. Augustine, the disorder that exists in nature is ultimately traceable to this initial act of disobedience. The Devil is also the one who leads human beings into the self-righteousness that turns us against God in our pride and arrogance. The Devil thus represents an inescapable aspect of the human condition that drives us away from God, and it is only the recognition of our helplessness against this condition, Luther believed, that can ultimately lead us back to God. We need to understand the term *Anfechtung*, then, as describing a fundamental element of Christian life, one dominated by the Devil, but also a source of faith. The term continued to be used in this sense into the seventeenth century,[61] and it was understood in this way by Melchior

---

[59] See Scaer (1983).

[60] Such a belief is called "providentialism," meaning that all things, positive and negative, are the direct product of God's divine providence. For a discussion of this doctrine in demonology, see Clark (1997, pp. 445–56).

[61] It is found, for example, in Johannes Neser (1617, pp. 51–83).

Neukirch in his description of Appolonia's possession, and most likely by the legal faculty at the University of Helmstedt in their *Gutachten* concerning Elizabeth Lorentz. With this idea of *Anfechtung* in hand, therefore, we can look more closely at the role of the Devil in the two cases of Elizabeth Lorentz and Appolonia Stampke.

9. THE DEMONIC PACT

The crime of which Elizabeth Lorentz was suspected was that she had formed a pact with the Devil, who was thought by Christians of Elizabeth's time as the first and most powerful of a host of demons, or fallen angels.[62] The idea of a diabolical pact first appeared with Augustine of Hippo (354–430). Christians in the first centuries after Christ believed that the gods of the pagan Greeks and Romans were demons, and so all forms of pagan worship came to be seen as devil worship. Augustine added to this the idea of a demonic pact: an agreement between a human and a demon, whereby the human pledges his soul to the demon and against God in exchange for some service. According to Augustine, all magic relies on such a demonic compact, since human beings are unable to produce magical effects through their own powers.[63]

From its association with magic, the idea of a pact with Satan became a central component of the idea of witchcraft in the late Middle Ages. The charge of a diabolical pact was first made against magicians in the aristocratic courts, especially necromancers, whose activities worried church authorities.[64] Worship of the Devil was also a charge brought against heretical movements such as the Cathars and the Waldensians in the twelfth through fourteenth centuries. Over time, the idea of the magician's pact merged with that of devil-worshipping heretics, to form the composite idea of witchcraft.[65] According to this conception, witches formed a collective host of practitioners of maleficent magic, who raised terrible storms and caused illness and death in people and animals. They were believed to gather regularly at *sabbats*, orgies of blasphemous and grotesque rituals.[66]

---

[62] The word "demon" comes from the Greek, *daimon* or *daimonion*, which in Hellenic pagan culture referred to beings that mediate between humans and the gods. Satan (in Hebrew, the Adversary) does not appear in the Hebrew Bible as an evil spirit but as an instrument of God, carrying out trials of God's people. Christians in the first decades after Jesus's crucifixion adopted the figure of Satan as the enemy of God's kingdom with a host of lesser demons at his command. For the early history of the Devil, see Almond (2014, pp. 1–30) and Levack (2013, pp. 32–55).

[63] See Augustine of Hippo (1958, Book II, Chapters 20–24).

[64] Kieckhefer (1989, pp. 176–201) and Peters (2001).

[65] The best overall introduction to the idea of witchcraft in early modern Europe is Levack (2006).

[66] On the origins of belief in the *sabbat*, a classic study is Cohn (1993).

At the *sabbat*, witches were believed to form a pact with the Devil through a formal allegiance, the making of which was their chief spiritual crime. In this act, witches renounced their faith in God and pledged themselves to the Devil as his servant in return for magical powers.[67] These ideas took a long time to coalesce; the composite image of diabolical witchcraft reached its final form only in the first half of the fifteenth century. In written works, it made its first complete appearance in the 1430s in a book called *Formicarius* (*The Ant Hill*), written by a Dominican church reformer, Johannes Nider.[68] After this publication, the idea spread rapidly and many books were printed in the fifteenth century expanding and promulgating it. The most famous of these was the *Malleus Maleficarum* (*The Hammer of the Witches*) of 1486 by a Dominican inquisitor, Heinrich Kramer (c. 1430–1505).[69] Over the next two centuries many thousands of people were executed for the crime of diabolical witchcraft, most of them women.[70]

It is the idea of a diabolical pact that connects the trial of Elizabeth Lorentz with the crime of witchcraft. The principal concern of the Brunswick court was that she had made a pact with the Devil, as evidenced in her exchange of fingernail clippings for seeds. Yet as was suggested in Section 1 above, Elizabeth does not fit the idea of a witch perfectly. She is never described in the trial records as a witch, nor did the court actively pursue the possibility that she practiced magic, nor did they suspect her of attending the witches' *sabbat*. Whatever Elizabeth might have been suspected of, it was not witchcraft in its full sense of a diabolical sect bringing destruction upon the world.

There is, however, a key element of diabolical witchcraft that does appear in the testimony of Elizabeth Lorentz beyond the suspicion of a diabolical pact: that of sexual seduction by the Devil. From the mid-fifteenth century, virtually all writers on the dangers of witchcraft asserted that witches had carnal relations with Satan. Authors of demonological texts argued that women were particularly susceptible to witchcraft because of their sexual appetite, which the Devil exploits to lure them into a pact. In one of the more infamous passages of the *Malleus Maleficarum*, Kramer writes, "Everything is governed by carnal lusting, which is insatiable in

---

[67] It was believed that witches had no power for magic themselves, and that it was the Devil who brought about the apparent magical effects through his superior natural abilities. Demonic magic, therefore, was thought to be entirely illusory although the harm it produced was real.

[68] See Bailey (2003).

[69] For an English translation of the *Malleus Maleficarum*, see MacKay (2009).

[70] Morton and Dähms (2017) contains a bibliographical essay on the historical literature on the trials.

them" (MacKay 2009, p. 170). According to the court records, the idea that the Devil wanted sexual intercourse with Elizabeth Lorentz was first raised by Anna Geitel, and later by the court. In answer, Elizabeth said that the Devil came to her in the form of a well-dressed young man who wanted to have intercourse with her. To the court she testified that the Devil "expected indecency from her," which clearly meant sex, but she says that he only kissed her several times. Here again, however, the charge of witchcraft does not fit the trial of Elizabeth Lorentz perfectly. While there was suspicion of sex with the Devil, neither the questioning of the court nor Elizabeth's testimony suggest anything like orgies of unnatural sex that appear in the more infamous of the witch trials. The sexual element of the trial of Elizabeth Lorentz occurs as a form of temptation, an allurement that Elizabeth is attracted by but resists.[71] The Devil in the guise of tempter appeared in Christian literature from its very beginnings. The Christian martyr of the fourth century, St. Juliana of Nicomedia, fought with the Devil in the form of an angel of light, and St. Benedict, one of the founders of the monastic tradition, was tempted by the Devil in his hermitage with a beautiful young woman.

Given the similarity between Elizabeth's sexual temptation and the legends of the saints, we can perhaps approach the topic of diabolical pacts from this angle as well. Such pacts appeared occasionally in medieval descriptions of the lives of the saints (or hagiographies) collected to serve as *exempla*, models of pious or ethical life.[72] The most widely distributed such collection was *Legenda Aurea* (*The Golden Legend*), compiled around 1260 by Jacobus da Varagine, Archbishop of Genoa (1230–1298). Among these stories were some that told of men who formed pacts with the Devil in exchange for earthly reward and who were redeemed through divine mercy. One widely circulated tale concerned St. Basil of Caesarea: a servant of a very pious man was caused by the Devil to fall in love with the daughter of his master, for whom her father had chosen a life of chastity. In his passion for the girl the young servant sold himself to the Devil, and with his help he married her. But the trick was exposed when the young man could not enter a church, whereupon the girl took him to St. Basil, who forced the demon to return the pact. Another such legend is that of a certain Theophilus, a saintly priest of Chartres in the sixth century who

---

[71] Johnstone (2004) argues that Protestant ideas of the Devil in early modern England were concerned with temptation rather than the inversion of the moral and divine orders suggested by the image of witchcraft. However, the temptations in Johnstone's study are internal, unlike Elizabeth's handsome young man.

[72] On this topic, see Seiferth (1952).

was chosen for a bishopric but who, in his modesty, declined the honor. The Devil assailed him, however, and filled him with ambition so that he signed a pact in exchange for the bishopric he had earlier renounced. Soon, however, he felt great remorse for his sin and called upon the Virgin Mary. She instructed him to renounce his pact and confess his sin to Christ, and, when he had done this, Mary returned the pact he had signed and laid it on his breast.

Both of these legends appear in a remarkable body of work composed in the tenth century by a Benedictine nun named Hrotsvitha (c. 935–c. 973), in the cloister of Gandersheim (which is coincidentally quite close to Brunswick).[73] The tenth century is viewed by some as the darkest part of the Middle Ages, when learning and literacy were at their lowest ebb. Yet Hrotsvitha wrote a large number of Latin literary works of high quality: eight verse legends, six dramas, and a collection of historic poems, which were rediscovered in the fifteenth century and widely published thereafter.[74] Her verse recounting of the stories of St. Basil and Theophilus gives us insight into the ways in which these tales were understood in the Middle Ages. Although the stories involve demonic pacts, Hrotsvitha's purpose in composing her verses was to demonstrate the mercy of Christ. The message was that no matter how serious the sin, even an explicit signing of a pact with the Enemy, it will be forgiven if the remorse of the sinner is genuine. In the legend of St. Basil, the saint tells the young servant, "The only son of the father, the most meek judge of the world, who has never despised anyone converted to him, if you will bewail your fault, rejoices to grant assistance" (Wiegand 1936, p. 203). Similarly, after Theophilus's conversion, the bishop of Chartres says, "Come, hasten hither in joy all you faithful ones, and, praising the kindly deeds of God with loyal hearts, believe that God, merciful in his goodness, never rejoices in the destruction of the wicked, but rather wills to give life everlasting to those returning to him" (Wiegand 1936, p. 181). The Devil in these legends is the origin of the sins committed by these young men, yet he cannot overcome the mercy of Christ, invoked through the pleas of St. Basil and the Virgin Mary.

Six hundred years after Hrotsvitha, a derivative of the legend of Theophilus had a very different ending and a different moral message. One of the most popular books of late sixteenth-century Germany was the anonymous *Historia von Dr. Johann Faustus* (*Legend of Dr. Johann Faustus*), printed by Johann Spies in 1587, which served as the model for the famous

---

[73] We are grateful to Rosalind Lintott for drawing Hrotsvitha to our attention.
[74] See Hrotsvitha (2001). For English translations, see Price (2015), and see Wiegand (1936) for Latin and English side by side. For critical discussions, see Brown and Wailes (2013), Wailes (2006), and Brown, McMillin, and Wilson (2004).

Faust plays of Christopher Marlowe and Johann Wolfgang von Goethe.[75] In Spies's work, the young medical student, Faustus, becomes filled with a lust for knowledge and turns to the magical arts. In his quest, he conjures the demon Mephistopheles and enters into extended negotiations, after which he signs a pact in his own blood, pledging his body and soul in exchange for the spirit doing all that he demands for twenty-four years. Like Theophilus, Faustus comes to realize the folly of his pact, but unlike his predecessor he is told by Mephistopheles that he cannot be saved by any means whatsoever. Faustus is taken by Mephistopheles to all corners of the earth; he has many fabulous adventures (including stealing the Pope's dinner and having sex with all of Mohamed's concubines), and learns all the secrets of heaven and earth. But at the end of the twenty-four years his body is torn asunder by the spirit, and he is cast into everlasting hell (but not before warning a group of Wittenberg students of the tragic fate that can befall them). Whereas Hrotsvitha used the legend of Theophilus to illustrate Jesus's infinite mercy and forgiveness, the author of the *Historia* used the story of Faustus to draw a contrasting conclusion: those who in their arrogance abandon God and turn to the Devil can expect no more mercy from God than was given to Lucifer himself. Christ the redeemer is entirely absent in the book of Faustus.

As Frank Baron (1978) has shown convincingly, the shape of the legend of Faustus can be traced to Martin Luther and his close collaborator, Philip Melanchthon (1497–1560). The figure of Faustus was based upon a historical person named Georg Helmstetter, born in 1466. Helmstetter obtained the degree of master of philosophy at the University of Heidelberg, and under the name of Faustus he appears to have had a successful career as an astrologer. But Faustus was boastful, and from his pride he gained many enemies, one of whom was another astrologer, Joachim Camerarius (1500–1574), who had studied in Wittenberg and became an ardent follower of Luther. According to Baron, the image of Faustus as a diabolical magician came to Luther and Melanchthon via Camerarius. In 1538, Luther was directly involved in another case of a demonic pact, involving a student of Luther's own university named Valerius Glockner. The mention of this case in Luther's published *Table Talk* indicates that Luther scolded the boy so that he converted and resolved to become the Devil's enemy.[76] Fifteen years later Melanchthon gave a new version of the events, in which the boy signed a pact in blood in exchange for money. These two stories, of Faustus and Glockner, merged together in a further elaboration in 1585, in which

---

[75] A critical edition of the *Historia* is Riedl (2006).
[76] See Baron (1992, pp. 115–19).

a pact for twenty-four years is included.[77] This book was a direct source for Johann Spies's *Historia* of 1587, which permanently fixed the legend of Faustus as a diabolical sorcerer.

There is, then, a question about the extent to which the idea of a diabolical pact in the *exempla* tradition can be usefully applied to the case of Elizabeth Lorentz. She was certainly not a diabolical sorcerer. It would appear that in their *Gutachten* the Helmstedt legal faculty saw her as a victim of the Devil rather than one who, like Faustus, sets out in pride and self-importance to make a pact with the Devil. As such, she more closely resembles figures like Theophilus, whose character is pure but who is lured by Satan into defiance of God. Here again, there is the suggestion of diabolical temptation rather than a willing alliance with Satan.

10. DEMONIC POSSESSION

A second representation of diabolical *Anfechtungen* is demonic possession. The bodily possession of human beings by demons appears many times in the New Testament in stories of exorcism by Jesus and later by his disciples.[78] The demons of the Gospels violently take over the bodies of their victims, causing seizures and convulsions, and speaking with demonic voices.[79] Belief in possession, and the means used to rid people of possessing spirits, changed dramatically over the time between the first centuries after Christ and the years of the Reformation. The Gospel exorcisms represent an element of Jesus's miraculous ability to heal the sick, and the stories emphasize his power to drive out the demons, providing vivid demonstrations of his divine nature. Indeed, as Nancy Caciola (2003, p. 36) points out, the demon in Mark 1:23–24 recognized Jesus as the "Holy One of God" long before the disciples did. As Christianity expanded in late Antiquity and the early Middle Ages, the power to exorcize demons also became an important element of the lives of the early saints.[80] Marek Tamm (2003, p. 22) suggests that exorcism was the *sine qua non* of sanctity in medieval times. The earliest of these saintly exorcism stories occurred in the hagiographies of the saints of late Antiquity, such as St. Martin of Tours (316–397). In these tales, demoniacs are cured of their condition by the saints just as Jesus healed the sick in the

---

[77] Hermann Witekind, *Christlich bedencken und Erinnerung von Zauberey*. See Baron (2009).
[78] Belief in demonic possession seems to have been common in Jewish communities in the centuries before Jesus. See Levack (2013, pp. 50–52) and Almond (2014, pp. 1–8).
[79] For a useful summary of the five most detailed exorcism stories in the New Testament, see Levack (2013, pp. 32–40).
[80] See Frankfurter (2010) for descriptions of the early stages of this development, during which demons were often associated with the pantheon of pagan spirits.

Gospels (Newman 1998, p. 739). Possession and exorcisms became common again in the thirteenth century, and the saints of the Middle Ages (especially St. Francis of Assisi, St. Dominic, and St. Bonaventure) were also renowned for their abilities (Levack 2013, p. 95). In the medieval hagiographical literature, exorcisms became struggles between the saint and the demon, and often the exorcist was forced to try different means to expel the spirit, using the sign of the cross, prayer and holy water, wine or bread, and importantly formal adjurations. These exorcisms were generally difficult, and the demons might be chased through the body, return to the body of the victim, or enter another person's body.[81] The events thus represented battles between the divine and the demonic.[82] After their deaths, the saints' relics or their shrines were believed to possess the power of what Tamm calls "post-humous exorcism" (2003, pp. 16–17). Relics included hair and other body pieces, which were placed on the victims' head or mouth, and in some cases included the soil onto which the water used to wash the body of the deceased saint had been poured out.[83]

Another stage in the development of exorcism in the Western church came in the fifteenth century, on the eve of the Protestant Reformation. Exorcism before that time had largely been the domain of saintly miracles, and the techniques for exorcisms were *ad hoc* or borrowed from whatever materials were to hand (Kieckhefer 1989, p. 73). But in the fifteenth century the priest rather than the saint became the central figure in the battle against the demonic. In addition, exorcisms became increasingly formalized as part of the church's semi-official liturgical practices (Caciola 2003, pp. 231–43). Rituals and formulas were developed for both the identification of spirits and exorcism itself, and some of the formulas involved the use of demonic language—patterned, rhythmic strings of syllables—to communicate with and command the demons. Manuals of exorcism were produced in large numbers, some in pocket book form, for use by priests in their local diocese, directing their efforts against the demonic. The changes in exorcism appear to have been produced during what Nancy Caciola has called a "crisis of authority" in the late medieval church. Given the difficulties faced by the church in the late Middle Ages, which we mentioned earlier, the church needed ways to reassert itself against pressures both from within the hierarchy of the church and from the demands of reform movements among the laity. One of the means by which the church reaffirmed its authority was by appropriating the exorcism of demons and absorbing

---

[81] For a demon chased through the body, see Caciola (2003, p. 47).
[82] The four illustrations in Tamm (2003, pp. 10–11) are vivid images of these struggles.
[83] For the latter, see Raiswell and Dendle (2008, p. 278).

it into its liturgical practices. Caciola (2003, pp. 248–49) argues that the rituals and use of demonic language demonstrated priestly mastery over the demons, forcing them to identify themselves and commanding them to return to their proper place in the cosmological order. In ways such as this, during a period of instability, the official church used the domain of exorcism to assert its authority over spiritual elements of communal life.[84]

By the middle of the fifteenth century, however, these formal, ritual-istic exorcisms became the target of attack by critics of the church. One reason for this was the fact that rituals for exorcism were in many ways indistinguishable from those used in necromancy, the magical practice of summoning demons (Kieckhefer 1989, pp. 166–68).[85] Criticisms of formal exorcisms took a dramatic turn with the advent of the Protestant Reforma-tion. Martin Luther and later reformers took the similarity between magic and exorcism to be indicative of a much larger problem within the Catholic Church, arguing that a great many of its rites and ceremonies were simply forms of superstition that the Devil had introduced in the days since the early church.[86] Taking Scripture as unassailably factual, Luther believed that possession was common in the days of the apostles and that the bibli-cal exorcisms were necessary to establish the faith. Yet he argued that since those days exorcisms had become a tool of the Devil, a means through which he cooperated in the schemes of the papacy, pretending to be driven out by the false rituals of the church. The Devil is never forced to leave by these ceremonies, Luther claimed, but rather left voluntarily in order to lure people into the superstitious belief that such rites were sacred. This criticism fit with the common Christian doctrine that the Devil is a master of disguise and often appears as an "angel of light" (2 Corinthians 11:14). In his sermons on Matthew 5, 6, and 7, Luther exclaimed, "Who could list all the knavery done in the name of Christ or Mary to drive out devilish spirits?" (Luther 1955–2016, vol. 32, p. 525).[87] Where the Catholic Church used exorcisms to demonstrate the power of God and the church over the Devil, Protestants took them as examples of demonic deceit and the errors of the Catholic faith.

---

[84] In the later Middle Ages, possession by evil spirits became entangled with possession by the Holy Spirit. This problem was especially acute in cases of intensely devout women who expe-rienced extraordinary visions. See Newman (1998), Caciola (2000) and (2003), Sluhovsky (1996), and Blumenfeld-Kosinski (2010 and 2015).

[85] Kieckhefer (1989) finds that in many texts the terms "exorcise," "conjure," and "adjure" were used interchangeably.

[86] For a detailed history of church responses to superstition and its role in the struggle between Catholics and Protestants, see Cameron (2010).

[87] Quoted in Midelfort (1999, p. 97).

Luther was not skeptical, however, of the reality of possession and believed that there were as many cases in his day as in biblical times. Luther himself described many cases of possession, in some of which he was himself involved. He took the rise of possessions as a sign of the coming apocalypse and the impending victory of Christ, before which the Devil would expand his activities and Christians would be beset by doubt and fear. It was indeed true that possessions became much more numerous and dramatic in the sixteenth century. Demoniacs in biblical and medieval times suffered from trances and seizures, and possessed great bodily strength; they also beat themselves and wandered naked or in rags. But in the years of the Reformation, other symptoms appeared.[88] As well as exhibiting extreme bodily symptoms such as rigidity, contortions, and vomiting of foreign objects, demoniacs also spoke in languages unknown to them, experienced visions, and made clairvoyant declarations. Both Catholic and Protestant authors across the sixteenth and seventeenth centuries argued that these were signs of the coming End of Days foretold in the Book of Revelation.[89]

Given their shared conviction that demonic possession was linked to the apocalypse, the best Christian response to possession became a matter of intense and vociferous debate between the faiths. All sides in the debate used the issue to define their theology and liturgical practice, and to attack others as atheists or deluded by Satan. The Lutheran response to possession emphasized the doctrine that relief from Satan can be granted only by God, and it is granted to those who seek it with humility and gratitude, not through the powers of any created thing. Possession thus provided Lutherans with examples of the true purpose of *Anfechtungen*: to bring Christians to see their complete dependence on God and to recognize his mercy on those who seek his aid. No human capacity or ritual, even divinely inspired, can usurp the power of God to control and direct the elements of his creation. In the seventeenth century, the proper response to possession became part of numerous Lutheran books of moral conscience. This point is especially important in understanding the context of Appolonia Stampke, for her life and experiences occurred at the height of these contests between the Protestant and Catholic churches. We can end this section on possession with a passage from one such work, *A Treatise on Cases of Conscience*, by Friedrich Balduin (1575–1627):[90]

---

[88] Levack (2013, pp. 6–15) gives a list of common symptoms of possession in the early modern period.

[89] This literature is studied in detail in Stuart Clark (1997, pp. 401–22).

[90] See Balduin (1628).

What is to be done with the possessed? And can the devil be cast out by using a certain method?

1. Let experienced physicians be consulted as to whether [there is a medical explanation].
2. When a true possession is recognized, let the poor one be committed to the care of a minister of the Church who teaches sound doctrine, is of a blameless life, who does nothing for the sake of filthy lucre, but does everything from the soul.
3. Let him diligently inquire what kind of life the possessed one led up to this point, lead him through the law to the recognition of his sins. If he was previously pious, let him console him, that even God sometimes leaves His people in the power of the devil for certain causes, which the histories of Job and Paul testify.
4. After this admonition or consolation has taken place, let also the works of a natural physician be used, who will cleanse him from malicious humors with the appropriate medicines. For it has been ascertained that possessed people frequently suffer from a double disease, namely of body—from a melancholy humor—and of soul, for example, insanity, grief, weariness of life, desperation.
5. It is not necessary to bring him into the temple [church] in the sight of the people, as the custom is for many. Let the confession of the Christian faith be once required of Him, let him be taught concerning the works of the devil destroyed by Christ, let him be sent back faithfully to this Destroyer of Satan, Jesus Christ, let an exhortation be set up to faith in Christ, to prayers, to penitence.
6. Let ardent prayers be poured forth to God, not only by the ministers of the Church, but also by the whole Church. Let these prayers be conditioned, if the liberation should happen for God's glory and the salvation of the possessed person, for this is an evil of the body.
7. With the prayers let fasting be joined, see Matt. 17:21.
8. And alms by friends of the possessed person [should be given to the poor], Tobit 12:8–9.

In summary, all things happen by prayers and the Word.

If the [desired] effect does not immediately follow, remember that not even the adjurations of exorcists are always efficacious. And this benefit of going out [of the devil] is bodily, therefore in prayers of this kind, the will of God must always be included. Thus, He hears them

Figure 3 The melancholy temperament
Anonymous woodcut, 1483.

not according to our will but for our help [according to what's best for us]. But the fact that our prayers for the possessed are not heard immediately and as we ask is due, among other things, to the unbelief of the possessed ones, who do not approach with certain faith, asking liberation from God. Therefore, Christ said to the parent of a certain demon-possessed one, "If you can believe the liberation of your son, it will happen."[91]

These were the kinds of directions that Melchior Neukirch would have followed, especially the sixth. The fact that he compiled his book of prayers after his initial appeals to God did not work to relieve Appolonia of the Devil reflects the general summary at the end: God does not respond to our prayers according to our will, but according to what is best for us.[92]

---

[91] From an abridged Latin version of Balduin's text in Dunte (1664, pp. 100–1). Translation by Benjamin T.G. Mayes (2017, pp. 332–34). On Balduin, see Roderick Martin (2008) and Mayes (2016).
[92] Neukirch (1596b) uses the biblical story of the death and resurrection of Lazarus in John 11:1–44 to illustrate this claim.

The Lutheran response to possession thus changed the traditional pattern of exorcisms performed in the manner of Christ and the saints. Getting free of possession became for Lutherans a matter of submission to the will of God, rather than a demonstration of the power of sacred ritual. Further, Appolonia's symptoms were not typical of demoniacs in Catholic contexts. The initial effect that the possessing demon had on her is a loss of confidence in God's love and her own faith, just as Luther himself described the influence of the Devil. Through her ordeal she tried to attend sermons, to confess her sins, and to receive communion, but the Devil tried equally hard to prevent her in this. She did not suffer from a madness of the kind common to demoniacs in the Middle Ages, therefore, but from a struggle to maintain her Christian faith and practice.

11. MELANCHOLY

In the quotation from Balduin, the first point made is that physicians should be consulted to seek a medical diagnosis before turning to demonic explanations, and it includes the application of medicines for melancholy during the dispelling of the demon. As this example shows, during the Renaissance and early modern period, diagnosing and treating seizures, madness, and other extreme behavioral symptoms as medical conditions with natural causes coexisted with, and was often combined with, treatments of demonological causes.[93] This appears in the two cases translated in this book. The court in Sangerhausen suspected that Elizabeth was not of sound mind, and the Brunswick court investigated whether this might be the origin of her pact with Satan. Laurentius Gieseler dismissed the hypothesis that she suffered from melancholy, yet in the end the law faculty of Helmstedt determined that her pact with Satan was made while she was suffering mentally from his attacks. Similarly, Melchior Neukirch considered whether Appolonia Stampke suffered from an illness of the head or a "disorder of reason." Medical diagnoses of mental illness were not ignored, then, by those who investigated demonic interference in the early modern period.

The medical ideas that were applied during this period were extensions of theories formulated in the classical world of the ancient Greeks, Romans, and Arabs. The most influential medical explanation for symptoms of madness in the early modern period was melancholy.[94] The term is

---

[93] This subject has been extensively studied in Germany by H.C.E. Midelfort. See especially Midelfort (1999).

[94] Two other common diagnoses were epilepsy and hysteria. See Levack (2013, pp. 115–17 and pp. 123–29.)

from the Greek *melaina kholé*, meaning "black bile," from a medical theory attributed to the Greek physician Hippocrates (c. 460–c. 370 BCE), and expanded by the Roman physician Galen of Pergamon (129–c. 216) and the Arab philosopher and physician Avicenna (c. 980–1037). The theory explained human health as dependent upon a balance among four humors (or fluids): blood, yellow bile, black bile, and phlegm, associated with different organs of the body. As well as maintaining bodily functions, the humors were held to be responsible for differences between personalities, depending on which humor predominated in a particular person. The melancholic personality was prone to moodiness, solitude, and introspection. Imbalances in the humors produced illness, and a strong preponderance of black bile was thought to produce various forms of hallucination and madness.

In the early Middle Ages, medical ideas from Antiquity had little impact, with most commentators following the biblical tradition in which little distinction was drawn between cases of bodily possession, illnesses caused by the Devil, and illnesses with natural causes. With the recovery of classical literature beginning in the twelfth century, however, naturalistic explanations of madness began reappearing alongside the demonic, particularly in the universities.[95] The sixteenth century saw a resurgence of interest in classical ideas, and melancholy became a tremendously popular subject, both as a personality type and a disease, and hundreds of artistic and literary works, medical treatises, and doctoral dissertations on melancholy were produced in the sixteenth and seventeenth centuries.[96] Midelfort (1984 and 1999, pp. 140–81) claims that a significant change occurred in German medicine in the middle of the sixteenth century. He argues that in the early part of the century melancholy was not prominent as a medical diagnosis, and popular medical literature on madness generally combined herbal pharmacology with demonology. From the middle of the sixteenth century, however, physicians in the German universities began to replace the naive eclecticism of earlier treatments with the methods of classical medicine, applying Galenic techniques to new areas and new hypotheses. Among these physicians were some who interpreted all diseases, including mental illness, as purely physical in origin, even though a complete reduction of human behavior to the physical was at odds with the idea of human beings as moral agents with free will.

---

[95] See Levack (2013, pp. 112–38). The topic of demonic versus medical diagnoses in the early modern period occurs frequently in Clark (1997).

[96] A subject that lies outside this book is the theory of melancholic genius, originating with Aristotle and revived by Marcilio Ficino. See Schleiner (1991) and Klibasky, Panofsky, and Saxl (1979). See also Clark (2007, pp. 52–67) on melancholic hallucinations.

Midelfort (1984, pp. 114–15) stresses an important and curious coincidence in the late sixteenth and early seventeenth centuries: naturalistic medical explanations and treatments of mental disorders were rising at precisely the same time as a dramatic increase in cases of demonic possession. Appolonia Stampke's possession occurred in the middle of this period. It was also just at this time that witch-hunting in the German territories reached its greatest intensity, with large panics occurring in numerous places. As a result of this overlap of very different ways of thinking, the period was marked by controversy and clashes of ideas. Nothing better exemplifies this aspect of the period than the writings of the Dutch physician Johann Weyer (or Wier in Dutch) (1515–1588) and the fierce debates his work provoked. Weyer managed to combine an admiration for tolerant scholarly learning, which he gained from his teacher, Agrippa von Nettesheim (1486–1535), with a strong Lutheran belief in the overwhelming power of the Devil in human life. In 1563 he published a treatise, *De Praestigiis Daemonum* (*On the Illusions of Demons*), in which he attacked practitioners of magic but also argued that old women accused of witchcraft were not guilty of any pact with the Devil, because they were melancholic and no match for the deceptions of Satan.[97] His argument combined medical, religious, and legal reasoning. Where witch-hunters claimed that old women were most susceptible to the wiles of the Devil, Weyer contended that their senility and melancholy rendered them incapable of entering into any binding contract, arguing that they needed medical treatment and religious instruction rather than punishment.[98] On legal grounds he contended that no contract based on deception, such that one party can only lose, is ever valid; witchcraft, then, is legally impossible. He also argued on religious grounds that while the Bible has much to say about possession, its alleged references to witchcraft are mistranslations. And against necromancy he argued that demons can never be bound by the powers or actions of any human being. Weyer fiercely condemned the practice of necromancy, distinguishing the deliberate practices of learned magicians from the delusions of melancholic old women. Weyer's arguments against the punishment of witches prompted fierce responses, particularly from the French political theorist Jean Bodin (1530–1596).[99] Weyer's defense of those accused of witchcraft produced an extended controversy over

---

[97] A complete translation of Weyer's book is found in Mora and Kohl (1991).

[98] Notice that, although Weyer defended old women from the charge of witchcraft, his arguments nonetheless continued the general view that women are weaker in mind and body than men. He simply drew a different conclusion from this premise than did the witch hunters.

[99] See Bodin (1995).

the question whether melancholy was a sufficient ground for innocence of a crime. According to Midelfort (1988), over time this debate led to the development of forensic medicine.

When the Brunswick court officials asked Laurentius Gieseler whether Elizabeth Lorentz suffered from melancholy, they had the Galenic humoral condition in mind. However, for early modern Lutherans melancholy also had a spiritual dimension, a condition of the soul, and this approach may well have had a bearing on the court's consideration of her statements and behavior. For Martin Luther, melancholy was one of the many forms of spiritual *Anfechtung*. On this view, the despondency and madness of the melancholic were attacks of the Devil, and treatment of the condition was accomplished through practices that lift the spirit and drive off the Devil's attacks (Midelfort 1999, pp. 320–21). Lutheran pastors of the late sixteenth and early seventeenth centuries followed Luther in viewing melancholy as a spiritual malady. We can take as representative of these views the writings of the pastor Simon Musaeus (1529–1582), who studied under Melanchthon in Wittenberg. Musaeus applied to the subject of melancholy a close connection that Luther drew between *Anfechtung* and the First Commandment.[100] Luther poured an enormous amount of depth and importance into the commandment as a profound statement of Christian faith. According to his faith, the First Commandment admonishes Christians to place all their trust and hope in the hands of God alone. To attribute fortune or misfortune of any kind to oneself or to any agency other than God is thus to violate the commandment. In two works, *Useful Instruction on the First Commandment* of 1569 and *The Melancholy Devil* of 1579, Musaeus elaborates a detailed account of the relationship between melancholy and the First Commandment.[101]

Musaeus's argument in these works is that spiritual melancholy arises as the result of neglecting two contrasting virtues of the First Commandment: proper fear of God and proper faith in God. Here he draws a parallel between the causes of physical melancholy as treated by the physician and the origin of spiritual melancholy. In the case of the physical ailment, the decline of the body's natural warmth and moistness through the excess of black bile produces either complete aridity or complete coldness. Similarly, neglect of the First Commandment can produce either excessive fear or excessive confidence. "For fear without faith brings despair, and faith without fear brings arrogance" (Musaeus 1569, sig. C2v). There are two

---

[100] For Luther's views on the relationship between *Anfechtung* and the First Commandment, and Musaeus's use of it in explaining melancholy, see Kolb (1982).
[101] See Musaeus (1569) and (1579).

ways in which we can lose sight of the First Commandment. In good times, we are inclined to see our fortune as deriving from our own virtues, not recognizing our dependence on God and falling into sinful arrogance. In bad times, we come to despair of God, believing ourselves to be rejected or abandoned, and lose our trust in God's mercy and forgiveness. Musaeus, and potentially the Helmstedt legal faculty, would have understood the second of these conditions, melancholic despair of God's love and mercy, as the kind of *Anfechtung* that drove Elizabeth to call upon the Devil in her despair in Sangerhausen.

12. CONCLUSION

Elizabeth Lorentz's confessions and stories reflect many of the ideas of the Devil and his relations with human beings that were common to her time and culture. Understanding Elizabeth's confessions to her master and mistress, and to the court, demands attention to the specific religious climate in which she lived. The same applies to the reactions of the court, the medical examiner, and the legal faculty at Helmstedt. The questions that they ask and the manner in which her confessions are investigated were formulated according to the Lutheran understandings of both diabolical *Anfechtung* and mental illness in the seventeenth century. Yet Elizabeth's case does not fit easily into any of the standard categories of relations with the Devil of that time. She was not a witch, a demoniac, or a Theophilus, though she exhibited some of the characteristics of each. According to the physician who examined her, she did not behave in the manner of those suffering from melancholy, yet the court determined that she was "plagued by strong *Anfechtung* by the Evil Enemy." Hers is not, therefore, a straightforward condition typical of its time. We need to analyze her case carefully in light of the expectations she would have had of how the Devil interacts with human beings and in light of the categories the people around her would have used to understand her condition and respond appropriately to it. To this end the story of Appolonia, told by Neukirch in his book of prayers, gives us a more complete idea of how devout Lutherans of early modern Germany perceived the threat of the Devil in the lives of Christians. The surviving records and witness descriptions of events like the trial of Elizabeth Lorentz and Appolonia Stampke's possession offer us the best clues we have into a conceptual world different from our own but inhabited by people very much like us.

Figure 4 Brunswick from the east, 1749

Figure 5 Neustadt city hall, 1422

This is where the trial of Elizabeth Lorentz took place. The building
was destroyed and replaced in the eighteenth century.

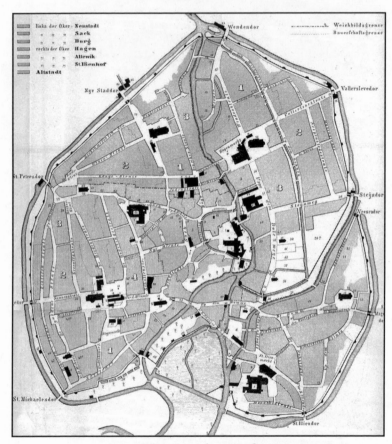

Map 1 Brunswick around 1400

This is a very early map of Brunswick, but it shows the municipality of
Neustadt very clearly in the northwest corner of the city. The cluster
of buildings in the center of the city is the ducal castle and cathedral
church of St. Blasius. To the west is the market place of Altstadt, with its
magnificent city hall and the Church of St. Martin, which was the center
of bourgeois power in the city. To the north of the castle is the Hagen
city hall, where the trial of Tempel Anneke took place (Morton and
Dähms 2017).

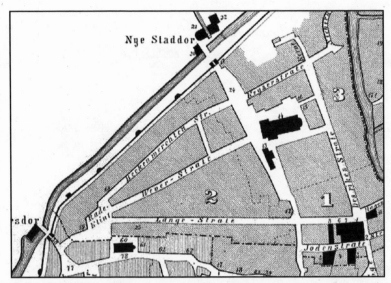

Map 2 Brunswick around 1400 (detail): The municipality of Neustadt
This is a detail of Map 1, showing the district where the events of this
book took place. The two gates to the city are St. Peter's on the left and
Neustadt at the top. Beckenwerder Strasse, where Elizabeth Lorentz
lived with the family of Hilmar von Strombek and Anna Geitel, is along
the city wall near the top. The Neustadt city hall, where the trial took
place, is in the lower right corner. The Church of St. Peter, the church
of Melchior Neukirch and Appolonia Stampke, is the smaller building
to the lower left. The Church of St. Andreas is the large building in the
center. Radeklint was the wheel-makers' market. Lange Strasse, where
Elizabeth found the warm bun, connects Radeklint with the Neustadt
city hall.

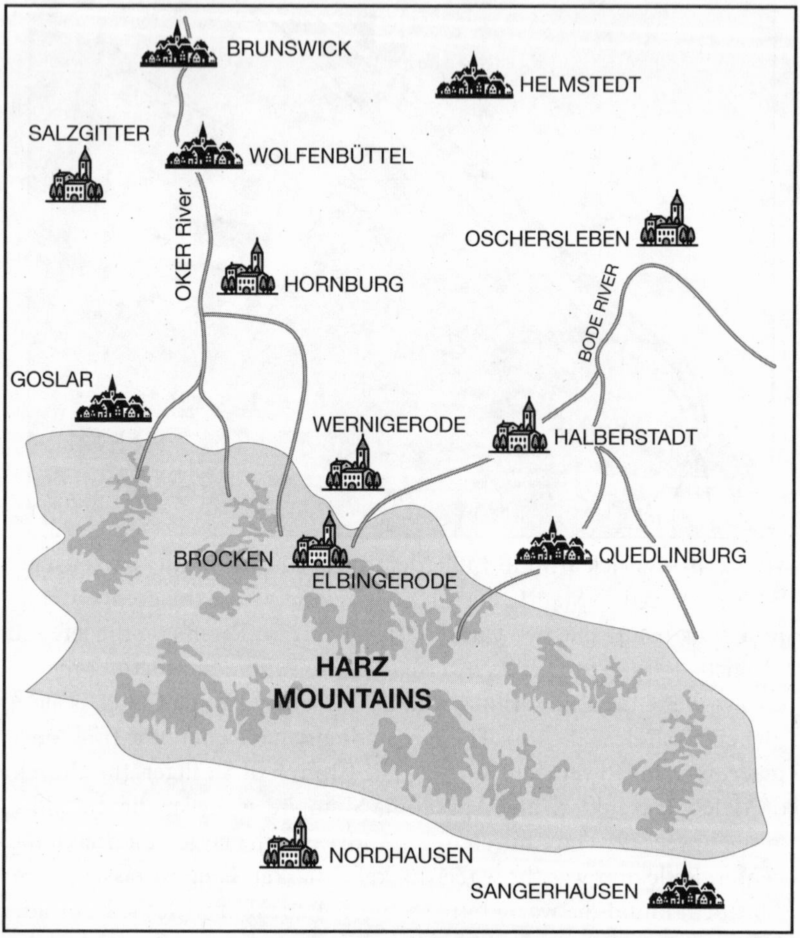

Map 3 Brunswick and region
This is a map of the region of Germany where the events of the book took place. Brunswick is in the top left corner, and Sangerhausen in the bottom right. To the northwest of Sangerhausen are the Harz Mountains, a steep and rugged terrain. Wolfenbüttel is south of Brunswick and Helmstedt is to the east.

Map 4 The Holy Roman Empire in 1648

The Empire was a large collection of principalities under the authority
of the emperor, but with very little unity. As shown on this map, the
principalities were divided among Catholic, Lutheran, and Calvinist faiths.
Brunswick in 1667 was an independent city situated within the territories
of the dukes of Brunswick-Wolfenbüttel. Both the city and the duchy were
Lutheran jurisdictions.

The Trial of Elizabeth Lorentz

Brunswick, Germany
20 December 1667–12 March 1668
Translated from Brunswick City Archive,
B IV 15b 32

[The trial record is 101 pages, divided by the court officials into sixteen folders (which we have called folios). Each folio has a cover page with a brief description of its contents.]

LIST OF PEOPLE

The Household of Hilmar von Strombek in Brunswick:

HILMAR VON STROMBEK THE ELDER, a brewer.
ANNA GEITEL, von Strombek's wife, also referred to as the *Strombeksche*.
JOHANN, two-year-old son of Hilmar and Anna.
ELIZABETH LORENTZ, a maid-servant.
MAGDALENA VORNEKE, a maid-servant.
ANDREAS, brew-master for Hilmar von Strombek.

Elizabeth's Family:

ANDREAS LORENTZ, Elizabeth's father, formerly a soldier in Brunswick, died around 1662.
ANNA TRIEBEL, Elizabeth's mother, living in Sangerhausen.
ELIZABETH'S SISTER (no name given), living in Brunswick.
BERND TRIEBEL, brother of Elizabeth's mother, with whom Elizabeth was employed before returning to Brunswick.

Officials of the Court in Brunswick:

Officers of the Court:

JOHANN SCHÜTZE, senior officer.
HEINRICH BAHRE.
JOACHIM GIERHARD.
JOCHIM ROHRBANDT.

Magistrates of the Court:

JOHANN VELHAGEN, magistrate for the municipality of Altstadt.
OTTO THEUNE, magistrate for the municipality of Hagen.
JOHANN PILGRAM, court scribe.
LAURENTIUS GIESELER, medical officer.
TWO JAIL GUARDS, one of whom is called Joachim Gödeke.
BAILIFF, who brings Elizabeth's skirt to the court, and is possibly the same
  whom Elizabeth accuses of assaulting her.
TWO PASTORS, who visit Elizabeth in her jail cell.

People in Brunswick and Wolfenbüttel, Mentioned in the Trial Records:

MAGISTER (MAGR.) SCHINDELER and MAGISTER CALVÖR, two
  pastors, whom Anna Geitel tried to persuade Elizabeth to visit after
  her initial confession.
JACOB MÖHLE, with whom Elizabeth's father was billeted and hence the
  family lived, before they left Brunswick.
JOHANN PHILIP RUMPFF, at whose house Elizabeth's sister resided.
CONRAD BRANDES, an apothecary in Brunswick, from whom Elizabeth
  was returning when she picked up the Devil's warm bun.
GESE LOHRENS, wife of Peter Soherling, who was imprisoned in
  Brunswick with Elizabeth.
ILSE WACHTMANN, a girl mentioned as being released from the
  Brunswick jail.
A BARBER in Wolfenbüttel, at whose shop Elizabeth's skirt was kept.
A WOMAN at Lehndorf, and a woman in Glieserode, who Elizabeth was
  said to seek for divining.
A WOMAN from *Friesen Strasse* in Wolfenbüttel, whom Elizabeth accuses
  of exposing her in Wolfenbüttel.

Officials of the Court in Sangerhausen:

CHRISTIAN WADELL, a member of the city council in Sangerhausen, who wrote to the Brunswick court concerning Elizabeth's imprisonment in Sangerhausen.

Court Officials:

HENDRICH APPEL VON LÜTTICHEN.
CHRISTIAN VORKIL.
MARTIN BRÜCKENCAMP.
MARTIN TILE, the executioner.

People in Sangerhausen (Possibly Fictional) Referred to in Elizabeth's Testimony:

A MAJOR, who Elizabeth says was executed for killing a nobleman.
A SMITHY WORKER, to whom Elizabeth says she was engaged.
A LINEN WEAVER'S APPRENTICE, who Elizabeth says was attracted to her.
A WHEEL-MAKER'S SON, with whom Elizabeth was said to be in love and with whom she may have become pregnant.
MARGRETHE MEISTER (also referred to as "the Meisterin"), whose child Elizabeth was accused of attempting to kill.
MILLER, who wanted to rape Elizabeth, and who she said she murdered.
A MILLER'S HELPER, with whom Elizabeth was accused of having a child, which Elizabeth was accused of murdering.

People in Sangerhausen:

SIEGMUND HEINRICH HOFFMEYER, granary official of Sangerhausen, with whom Elizabeth was employed before returning to Brunswick.
MARTIN SCHRADE, a stablehand for Siegmund Heinrich Hoffmeyer.
DOROTHEA BOHLMANN, a maid-servant in the household of Siegmund Heinrich Hoffmeyer.
ADMINISTRATOR OF HALLE, to whom Elizabeth's mother appealed to have Elizabeth moved to the court house in Sangerhausen before her trial there.
TWO BATH MOTHERS IN SANGERHAUSEN, who examined Elizabeth under oath to determine whether she had carried a child.
CHRISTIAN KOFFERHAUSEN, someone the court instructed Elizabeth to apologize to in Sangerhausen, for reasons that are not given.

FOLIO 1

[*In this folio is the record of the court's questioning of Hilmar von Strombek, Elizabeth's employer. The questions are missing from the file. Normally they are filed separately from the answers.*]

Inquisitio[102]
Concerning the arrested Elizabeth N.
In specie[103]
Hilmar von Strombek the Elder's testimony without torture

Actum Brunswick at the Neustadt city hall, the 20th of December, *Anno* 1667
Through the appointed officials.

On the order received from the honorable[104] council, Hilmar von Strombek, the elder of this name, is summoned and is admonished to speak the pure truth regarding his former servant, now under arrest, N. N.,[105] and her behavior. And he reported on this as follows,

1. That eight days after the previous Michaelmas,[106] he acquired a servant girl named Elizabeth N. to be in service in his house. When she had been in service with them about fourteen days or a bit longer, they heard that the person sometimes sighed during the night. Of which they thought nothing particular, even though she was lying in her room in the house together with the children, in the belief that it might be happening from her imagination in sleep,

2. but afterwards he heard that the mentioned maid sat in the living room and sighed several times, also she said with these words, to his housewife and to the other maid present, that she intended to do something, if only she had already accomplished it. This talk they also didn't understand in a bad way, and therefore didn't reflect on it or ask what she meant by it. Because of that, such sighing and talk continued to the present.

---

[102] "Investigation."
[103] "In particular."
[104] In the original: "E. E.," or *Eure Ehrenwürdige*.
[105] *Nomen nescio*: "name unknown." It isn't clear why this was used here.
[106] The Feast of St. Michael falls on September 29.

3. But afterwards the person let herself be heard, especially to the other maid, Magdalena N., that she had sat in chains and irons in Sangerhausen. Because the maid now revealed this to her mistress, the housewife of the witness, she took that as a reason to question the person herself about the Sangerhausen business.

4. She then repeated the matter in that way to him—that the maid had confessed to her, how earlier at Sangerhausen she had lain at one end of a post, and on the other side of the post or block a major had lain on his bedding and was fastened to it, each person on the leg; how then the mentioned major, an old man, /: *this was supposed to have been this summer* :/ was later executed because he was said to have killed a nobleman.

5. Now when they both were brought food, she got hardly any, but the major got better and then shared it with her.

6. From this the witness's housewife had cause to ask further, "Why had she been captured and locked up like this?" To which she then answered that a smithy worker, an only son of his parents, engaged himself to her, while she also made herself liked by a linen weaver's apprentice.

7. One time, when she met with the linen weaver in her mother's house, someone saw them sitting together, who went to the pub and told the smithy worker, and said: "You are sitting here, while your Lizzie is sitting right now with another so and so." Thereupon the other, the smithy worker, left the pub, fetched his dagger, and when he came with it to her and the linen weaver's apprentice, and found them sitting together, he stabbed him to death beside her or in her presence. In that way, she and the smithy worker were brought in, and the smithy worker was beheaded, but on the petition of others she was let go and exonerated.

8. Later it was told to him by his housewife, that once at night when the witness was not at home, she, *Captiva*, had sighed or called in a little or small voice: "Oh my leg, my leg" /: *so that now one almost believed, that the person was more in front of the room than in it* :/ for almost half an hour, if it didn't last longer. Because of that his housewife called to her often and asked her, "What is wrong with you?" But she was unable to wake her up. Because of that she inquired further the next morning: "What had been wrong with her during the night that she called out like that? Had her leg hurt her so much?" Of which the current *Captiva* knew nothing, nor did she want to know that at that time throughout the previous night she had sighed in that way.

9. On the 26th of November *anni currentis*,[107] as he remembers it, the
    witness was brewing, and because of that he came into his living room
    between five and four o'clock in the morning, he found her lying on
    the small bench in front of the sideboard in the living room. As this
    seemed to him a strange place to sleep, he asked her, and said that he
    thought that she was in bed, to which she answered that she had lain
    there as comfortably as on the bed. Even though he said to her that
    she should still go there, she however did not want to. Instead she lit
    herself a candle and sat down to spin, saying that she had not spun
    much the previous evening and the mistress might be angry about
    that.

10. The same day, between eleven and ten at midday, as he remembers,
    she sat with others in the living room spinning, and started to raise
    her right hand in front of her, looking at it and opening and closing
    it, and sighed, saying she wished she were as deeply under the earth as
    above, while looking at her brown hand, and with that let herself be
    heard that she was a grave sinner. At this his housewife felt compelled
    to talk to her, to tell her not to be so worried. She also asked further
    what was wrong with her? Whether perhaps she wanted to go to the
    wedding, which she had been told the previous Sunday can easily be
    permitted, and she mustn't sigh about that.

11. After this conversation, the current *Captiva* started and said: "Oh
    mistress! I would like to confide in you or say something to you, if
    you wouldn't repeat it to anybody." Because his wife felt uneasy about
    that, she replied to the maid that she might be able to keep quiet
    about it, but also that she might be unable to keep quiet. After he,
    the witness, came into the living room during this talk, they stopped
    talking about it, but when he went away again his wife continued
    the previous talk with the maid and inquired more specifically. Yet
    before the person was willing to divulge anything further, she started
    and said: "Well, if I were to tell you, something really mad, that is,
    something peculiar, might happen to me." When his housewife
    nevertheless urged her to let her know what was wrong with her,
    the current *Captiva*, Elizabeth, said freely and confessed that
    Satanas /: *God be with us all* :/ supposedly came to her in person as a
    well turned out young man.

12. As the witness's wife now asked further what his desire was, she
    answered: she was supposed to promise him that she would soon
    murder or kill someone. His housewife then asked further, what

---

[107] "Of that year."

else she was supposed to do, whether she was also supposed to have intercourse with him, which current *Captiva* answered with "Yes."

13. When his wife now inquired further whether he also brought some money, to this she answered again and said that he had promised to bring her something, but after she had first accomplished that. And the witness and his wife did not know if it was the murdering, the killing, the intercourse, or what else should be understood from that.

14. As all this was talked about between the two, the witness's wife insisted that she should calm down, and offered that she would go with her to *Magister* Schindeler and *Magister* Calvör.[108]

15. To this *Captiva* started and asked: "Mistress, now you probably recoil from me, now you will not want to keep me?" She, the witness's housewife answered and said: "Yes, you can easily think that. See that good people take you in, and I will also give you a pair of dresses to help." But to this she did not answer anything specific that the witness knew of, she couldn't bring herself to go with her to the pastors.

16. At the end of these conversations his housewife came out of the room with the little boy in great fear and shock, and told him, the witness, everything mentioned before. Because of that he went into the room, and when he saw that the oft-mentioned Elizabeth also entered and wanted to start spinning again, he talked to the same and said, she should stop, because she had already spun more at his house than was to his liking, and wished that she had never started. Upon this talk the person immediately left the room towards the attic holding a white piece of cloth in her hands. And when the witness soon followed her, he found her sitting on a sack holding her hands to her cheeks and sighing.

17. After this the witness asked her, for how long had she had dealings with Satan? To that she then answered and said: "Three weeks." As he asked further, "in which way she had fallen in with him, and in which way did he come to her," she answered that she was walking along *Lange Strasse*[109] in the evening and had wanted to go to the apothecary to fetch some cream to put on her foot. There on the *Lange Strasse* a warm bun was lying that smelled good to her, so that she couldn't leave the spot until she had eaten it all. And this bun had tasted very good, as if laurel berries and the like had been in it. On the third day after that he, Satan, came to her /: *She did not want to say where and in which place* :/ and asked what business she had with his bread, she

---

[108] Two pastors (see below).
[109] A main street in Brunswick. See Map 2, p. lvi.

should have left it lying there. As she revealed all this to the witness, in a pitiful voice, she walked back and forth in the attic and collected her things, and went downstairs with it again. When she then came into the living room again following this, the witness asked her again, "Where did she have her meeting—in the living room or the bed room? As it is dark at night?" She replied again, "At the place where they met there was light enough." When he further said and asked: "Well, so do you eat and drink together?" to that she said: "Yes." She was quite timid, and did not want to eat in the morning, midday, or evening, but all the time she sat and sighed, until she finally left the house. Then the witness was anxious that she might leave town by the Neustadt gate or by the Wenden gate and might get up to something else. Because of that he sent the other maid after her, who could not come near her because the current *Captiva* threatened to stab the same. Because of that he had to do without his brew master, Andreas N., for a while, take him out of the brewhouse and send him after her, who then found her at the Hagen market and noticed that she had a large pastry and wanted to give him a part of it, but which he refused, because he was familiar with everything that had happened. Nonetheless he brought her back into the house. After that the witness sent for her sister at Johann Philip Rumpff's house three times, who came, not this time but later. Because of that, the sister, current *Captiva*, went away, making it known that she wanted to remember her sister for that.[110] Yesterday morning, right after they woke up, she came back into his house, she almost did him violence there, and horribly berated both him and her.

FOLIO 2

[*This folio contained the record of the questioning of Anna Geitel, von Strombek's wife. The question numbers referred to are those from the questioning of von Strombek, which are missing.*]

The report of Mrs. Anna Geitel, Hilmar von Strombek's wedded house-wife, and what else was remembered at the time.

---

[110] In the original: *derentwegen die Schwester itzige Captive weggangen, mit vermelden das Sie es der Schwester gedenken wolte.* The first sister here is Elizabeth.

Actum Brunswick at the Neustadt city hall, the 20th of December, *Anno* 1667
Through the appointed officials.

Since it was discovered that what Hilmar von Strombek tells is partially related by his housewife, by name Mrs. Anna Geitel, she was also summoned and *gravia admonitione*[111] questioned about the content of the numbered §§ in his testimony.

How she left the first § the same in all respects, except she added that, as far as she can remember, the current *Captiva* sighed every night, and when she, the witness, asked her if maybe the mare /: εφιαλτηζ :/ rode her,[112] she answered and said "Yes."

In the same way, she also confirmed the testimony of her husband, Hilmar von Strombek, contained in §2, and added that she had understood from the current *Captiva*, which according to her story she was supposed to accomplish, was supposed to happen outside in another place. That is why the witness wondered less about it.

With the 3rd and 4th § she reported and testified the same as her husband had put forward, except she used the words "shoot dead" for "murder," specifically that the nobleman had been shot dead.

From the 5th § she varies in this way, that as far as the witness is aware, *Captiva* said nothing about her food, but rather said that the major had received nothing from which she did not get her share.

To the 6th and 7th § she reports the same as the housemaster, except that she adds *in fine*[113] that *Captiva* said that the smithy worker had done much towards her being released, but to the 6th § she remembers that she heard nothing from *Captiva* about being engaged, rather she had said that both the smithy worker and the other one had wanted her.

With the 8th § the witness remembers, further to what her husband testified, that earlier *Captiva* called out for a long time, but no voice was to be heard from her, until in the end she let out a small sound, with these words, "my leg, my leg!"

She confirms the 9th § that she had heard it that way as well, and adds that the person, the current *Captiva*, did not like going to bed in the evenings.

---

[111] "With a serious warning."
[112] In old German, English, Dutch, and Norse, "mare" or "maere" was a word for an evil spirit that rides on a person's chest in sleep, causing bad dreams, hence "nightmare." "εφιαλτης" (*ephiáltis*) is Greek for nightmare.
[113] "In the end."

To the 10th § she says that she saw well that at that time *Captiva* raised her hand and lowered it into her lap, and because the witness was always anxious that the person, the current *Captiva*, might fall into disrepute,[114] because of that she talked to her. Then *Captiva* finally broke out and said that she was a grave sinner /: *as Hilmar von Strombek might likely have already reported.* :/

With the 11th § the witness leaves it as her husband had put it forward, and remembers at the same time that she had had concerns for a long time, before she had wanted to ask the person properly about this matter. But at the same time in her conscience she could not ignore whether perhaps the child could be helped. It occurs to her further, she can't recall whether the current *Captiva* used the word *Satanas*, rather she always talked about a handsome young man who came to her.

With the 12th, 13th and 14th § she reported the same as her husband, differing only in that she didn't hear that the young man had intercourse with *Captiva*, but that he wanted to have intercourse with her. In addition, that she had not talked about *Magr.* Calvör, but only about *Magr.* Schindeler.

To what was contained *sub* 15th §, she adds that *Captiva* said: "When she leaves the house, what would people say?" and that to this the witness gave the advice that they would say that she was not able to get along with the other maid, that is why she left the house.

The other testimony, from §16 to the end, is really Hilmar von Stombek's own testimony, so it remains at that, even though the witness *ex relatione ipsius*[115] also knew and could testify to all of this. With, and indeed not without, the addition that *Captiva* came into her house yesterday morning with a bucket and was deeply embittered towards the witness, and talked continuously about hitting and stabbing, because the witness was the one who made the matter public, and it should not be forgotten that she went diligently and enthusiastically to church and sang religious songs evenings and mornings.

FOLIO 3

[*In this folio is the record of the questioning of Magdalena Vorneke, Elizabeth's co-worker in the von Strombek household.*]

The report of Hilmar von Strombek's serving maid without torture

---

[114] In the original: *in mißhelligkeit gerathen mügte.*
[115] "Relating to the same."

Actum **Brunswick at the Neustadt city hall, the 20th of December,** **Anno 1667**

Through the appointed officials.

Magdalena Vorneke, born in Appenrode, currently in service as a maid for Hilmar von Strombek the elder, *admonita*,[116] reports that she heard nothing from her former co-worker, the now imprisoned Elizabeth N., except that she had told how she had been courted and held dear by two men, and then one of them, the smithy worker, was beheaded. The current *Captiva* hadn't said more. What else the *Captiva* had done, how she whined and sighed day and night, and how she observed her hand, also how she revealed her concerns to the mistress, also what she had discussed with the master in the attic and later in the living room, the witness knew nothing about at all. She did not come to the living room nor come at night to the bedroom, where she would have been able to hear such things. Asked, what harm had the witness done to the current *Captiva* that she threatened to stab her to death? Says, she didn't know, had said no hurtful word to the *Captiva*. She guesses it came from the fact that she often had to light the fire and do similar tasks, because the witness could not do everything in the house by herself. She had been peevish and strange about everything.

Asked, what did the now imprisoned do yesterday at Hilmar von Strombek's, her employer's house? Says, the *Captiva* came into the house yesterday morning at eight o'clock in the absence of Hilmar von Strombek, and she told off the mistress horribly and severely, because her business had become public. The *Strombeksche*[117] shouldn't have told anyone. She was not at all happy with that, and shouted indiscriminately, now at the *Strombeksche*, now at Strombek himself, and now at the witness. But the current *Captiva* also blanched very much yesterday, when she saw the witness coming from the living room, and transformed her face so much that the witness was concerned that she might be overpowered or be harmed by the *Captiva*. That is why she went back into the living room and left the current *Captiva* standing there.

FOLIO 4

[This is the first questioning of Elizabeth Lorentz by the court. It was part of the initial investigation of the case, to determine whether or not there was

---

[116] "With a warning."
[117] Anna Geitel, as the wife of von Strombek.

*sufficient legal grounds for a proper trial in which the accused and witnesses
would testify under oath.*]

The report of the Captiva, Elizabeth Lorentz, without torture
The 23rd of December, Anno 1667

———

Actum in the Neustadt jail, the 23rd of December, *Anno* 1667

By the honorable Joachim Gierhard, court officer, and both magistrates
of the court.

Elizabeth Lorentz, the current *Captiva, admonita de veritate dicenda*,[118]
says she is now twenty years old and was born here in Brunswick. Her
father had been named Andreas Lorentz, was a former soldier here, and
was billeted at the Wenden moat with Jacob Möhle. Her mother, who is
still alive, is named Anna Triebel, born in Lautenthal. And when her father
was discharged here six years ago, he moved to Sangerhausen together
with his wife and the current *Captiva*, where he then died after about a
year. The mother, his widow, was still there in Sangerhausen. The parents
had put her in school in her youth to learn how to read. After the death
of the father, her mother put her into service with other people—with
Heinrich Siegmund,[119] granary official of Sangerhausen, she served about
a year. Afterwards with her mother's brother, Bernd Triebel, and with him
until fourteen days before past Michaelmas, after which she arrived here.
And in the beginning, she stayed at the {...} before that {...} staying at
Lunst[120] until eight days after Michaelmas, and then she went into service
and stayed with Hilmar von Strombek the Elder's on *Beckenwerder Strasse*.

Asked, why is it that she is sitting there so melancholically? Whether
there was something on her heart, she should reveal it and not be tortured by evil thoughts, especially as that rarely brings about something good?

Finally says, she is saddened in her heart, because the Thursday after the
past Easter she was innocently arrested by the honorable council at Sangerhausen /: *as if she had been pregnant and killed the child* :/ and was brought
to a terrible subterranean jail until her mother appealed to the administrator at Halle, then she was brought from the terrible jail to the civic office in
Sangerhausen. And when she had been jailed for eight weeks and could not

———

[118] "Admonished to tell the truth."
[119] Siegmund Heinrich Hoffmeyer. See Folio 7.
[120] This sentence is not legible.

be convicted of what she had been accused of, especially as she had been previously examined by two bath mothers under oath,[121] after she had been kept imprisoned for fourteen weeks by the honorable town and eight weeks at the castle,[122] she was freed again.

Asked, whether during her long imprisonment she didn't perhaps become impatient and brought a curse upon herself and damned herself?[123] She should say so voluntarily, so that her conscience could be saved and she could be helped otherwise.

Says, the great impatience caused by the lengthy imprisonment finally brought it about that at midnight when she was sitting in the evil town jail, she burst out that if God and people did not want to free her from the evil jail, so and so should help. Thereupon, the following day at twelve o'clock, the Evil Enemy appeared in the form of a man, dressed in blue, with feathers of many colors on his hat, and said to her, if she wanted to join with him, he would help her get out of there. *Captiva* did not reply to the Devil about that, as she was very frightened and fell down to the ground. After about half an hour, as she awakened and got up, she saw nothing but fire around her. Then she hit her breast with her hand, and prayed and called to God for mercy. She didn't hear further from the Evil Enemy at that place, until she was in service with Hilmar von Strombek about four weeks past Michaelmas of this year. And the same sent her to Conrad Brandes, the apothecary's, house to fetch turpentine oil, and when she was on the way back to her master's house she saw a bun lying on the ground near the church yard of St. Andreas. So she picked it up, and because the said bun gave off such a lovely smell she felt compelled to eat it all. Then, as she got to her master's house later, she revealed this to her mistress and her co-worker, the maid. She complained that after she had eaten the bun she felt a great deal of fear around her heart. But she was scoffingly called names by the mistress, who said she should be ashamed of herself, and should not have eaten the bun.

On the third day following, midday at eleven o'clock, the Evil Enemy came to her in the brew house in the form of a young man with white trousers and a grey jacket, with boots and spurs, a dagger at his side, wearing a black cap of fine linen, saying, because she had eaten his bread, now she was his own, he also came closer and closer to her, and was with her almost day and night, until she was brought here to the prison, where she felt no

---

[121] To determine whether she had had a child.
[122] The Sangerhausen castle was the site of a large number of witch trials between 1536 and 1710, from which it earned the name "witches' tower." See Wilde (2003).
[123] In the original: *und sich ettwa verfluchet, und Vermaledeyet.*

further *Anfechtungen*. But the Evil Enemy could not get so far with her that she had intercourse with him. Further, he had expected indecency[124] from her, [only that he had kissed her several times, there she felt from his touch that he was very cold.[125]] He wanted her to kill three people. For that he wanted to put something in a paper for her, which she should use for that, and administer it to them or give it to them. And when she had accomplished that, he would bring her money enough.

──────────── **FOLIO 5** ────────────

[In this folio, the earlier questioning of Elizabeth is continued.]

Continuatio
The interrogation without torture of Elizabeth Lorentz
The 24th of December, *Anno* 1667

──────

Actum in the Neustadt jail, the 24th of December, *Anno* 1667
Through the appointed officials.

Following the initial *Examini* and interrogation without torture of Elizabeth Lorentz, which began yesterday, she is further questioned without torture, and specifically questioned whether she had been imprisoned in Sangerhausen and why?

Says, yes, at Sangerhausen, at the civic office, for this reason, that she was suspected of having killed a child. She was supposed to have become with child by her neighbor's son, a wheel-maker, a young man with whom she was in love *insciis parentibus*.[126] Nevertheless she was released again, because nothing was proven against her. She was not even once frightened by Martin Tile, the executioner there, nor had she met the same.

Asked, whether she was not loved for a time by a smithy worker and a linen weaver, and the first stabbed the other to death, and she was arrested because of that.

---

[124] The German term here is *unzucht*, which in this context clearly meant sex, although it could also refer to all manner of indecent behavior.
[125] This is a marginal insert. The original writing is crossed out and illegible.
[126] "Without the knowledge of her parents."

Says, no, rather that was the reason that it was said of her that she had killed a child.

Further asked, why then did she report to the *Strombeksche*, her mistress, what she described of the smithy helper and the linen weaver?

Says, they questioned her this way and that way, and she believed that she didn't owe it to everybody, especially those in the house, to tell the real truth about what her misfortune had been, why she had been jailed. But that the major was jailed together with her in a room, and later executed because he was supposed to have killed a nobleman.[127] Furthermore, she confesses, but with lowered eyes and hanging head, also with a quiet tongue and in a depressed voice, that Satan had expected her to kill the child of her master Strombek, but this she could not possibly do. And because she had only one day left to gather the resolve for it, she was unable to keep silent any longer, but revealed to her mistress that she was supposed to kill someone, yet she did not report anything about the child. But she still had not started a relationship with him, also she had no *Anfechtung* in the jail. Except when the *Examen* was held yesterday, it appeared to her that a black cat walked back and forth in the room, stroked itself against her, came at her from behind as if it wanted to jump at her /: *as the court officer, the honorable Jochim Rohrbandt, had noted about her movements, that she constantly looked around herself* :/ [which nonetheless really did not happen].[128] And her heart hurts so much, and she is in so much fear, that because of this she is unable to hold a book in her hands and read it.

She did not have a relationship with him nor anything to do with him [except that he kissed her, because she had been too weak for him; she had not eaten with him![129] even though he often pinched her very hard because of that; it is also now impossible for her to shed a tear. And she is heartily sorry that she has been led astray by him as far as she has reported. If only she were free of him from now on, and he would not attack her badly any further, now that she has revealed it *et ingemuit*.[130]

In the beginning of the *Examinis* the head of the *Captiva* was hanging very low, and she started and said she was damned regardless, because she had cursed herself so horribly.

---

[127] This sentence is left incomplete.
[128] The last comment is a marginal insert.
[129] This is a marginal insert.
[130] "and she moaned."

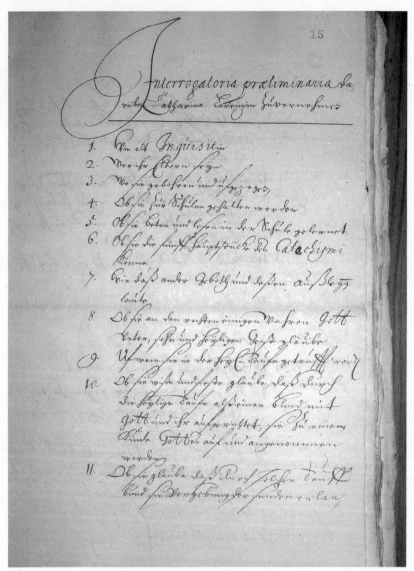

Figure 6   First page of Folio 6
Questions to be put to Elizabeth Lorentz.

FOLIO 6

[Here the court lists a set of thirty-one questions that are to be put to Eliza-beth, much of which covers the same ground as in her previous testimony. Her answers are recorded in Folio 7. That they are described as preliminary

questions indicates that this is still part of the first stage of the trial, to determine the degree of suspicion against the accused.]

Interrogat. praeliminaria[131]

___

Interrogatoria praeliminaria about which Catharine[132] Lorentz is to be questioned

1. How old is *Inquisitin*
2. Who are her parents
3. Where was she born and raised
4. Whether she was sent to school
5. Whether she learned to pray and read in school
6. Whether she knows the five principal parts of the catechism[133]
7. What is the Second Commandment and its meaning?
8. Whether she believes in the one single true God: Father, Son, and Holy Spirit
9. In whose name was she baptized in the Holy Baptism
10. Whether she knows and firmly believes that through Holy Baptism a pact was established between God and her, and that she was taken and accepted as a child of God
11. Whether she believes that through such a baptismal pact she has attained forgiveness of sins, and that because of this if she stays consistently in the proper true faith she is capable of partaking in eternal life through the merit of her Savior
12. Whether she knows during *Anfechtungen* how to console herself with this baptismal pact with God
13. Whether to this time Satan has afflicted her badly with *Anfechtungen*
14. When had she first noticed this seduction[134]
15. Whether he expected her to break her baptismal pact and to join herself to him
16. When, where, and how did it happen
17. Whether she agreed to do that

___

[131] "Preliminary questions."
[132] They mean Elizabeth.
[133] The Ten Commandments, The Apostles' Creed, The Lord's Prayer, Holy Baptism, and the Sacrament of the Eucharist.
[134] In the original: *Verführung*.

18. How had she acted otherwise towards him, and in which way did she fight him off or turn him away
19. Whether her melancholy might have originated from a grave vice and evil deed that she committed
20. Whether she was imprisoned in Sangerhausen
21. For what reason, and whether it didn't occur out of suspicion concerning her having committed the murder of a child
22. Whether she didn't continuously fornicate carnally with a male person there
23. Who is he
24. Whether she had been pregnant
25. /: *Si negat* :/[135] If she hadn't appeared suspicious or was thought to be pregnant, how did it happen that she was arrested as a child-murderer
26. Whether she perhaps killed or intended to kill other people's children
27. How was she released from jail in Sangerhausen
28. Whether she had the intention to kill Hilmar von Strombek's child
29. On whose initiative or order was she supposed to do this
30. What happened to her during her sleep at Hilmar von Strombek's, so that she whined and lamented so pitifully
31. When she was weighed down with melancholy, why did she not reveal this to a pastor or a father confessor

---

FOLIO 7

[These are the answers given by Elizabeth to the questions in Folio 6. In the original document the questions are not repeated. We have added them for convenience.]

The reply given, without torture, by the *Captiva* Elizabeth Lorentz to the *Interrogatoria praeliminaria* formulated in *Actis Num*. 6.

——

Actum Brunswick in the Neustadt jail, the 31st of December, *Anno* **1667**
    Through the appointed officials here.

---

135 "If she denies this."

Upon the received order the imprisoned Elizabeth Lorentz is interrogated without torture *gravia admonitione seria*[136] about the *Interrogatoria praeliminaria* formulated in *Actis Num.* 6. And the same testified as follows, which was written down verbatim.

Ad 1. *How old is Inquisitin,*

Says, twenty years.

2. *Who are her parents,*

Says, Andreas Lorentz, for twenty-four years a city soldier here, until he moved from here to Sangerhausen, where he died as a blacksmith and burgher, as this was mentioned at his memorial service. Her mother is named Anna Triebel and still lives in Sangerhausen, she helps with other people's work and makes lace.

3. *Where was she born and raised,*

In the city of Brunswick, which includes six years that she spent in Sangerhausen.

4. *Whether she was sent to school,*

Says, yes, here in Brunswick.

5. *Whether she learned to pray and read in school,*

Says, yes.

6. *Whether she knows the five principal parts of the catechism,*

Says, yes.

7. *What is the Second Commandment and its meaning,*

Says, you should not take the name of God the Lord in vain. Because the Lord will not leave the one who misuses his name unpunished.

Asked, what does that mean? To that she recites: we are supposed to fear and love God, so that with his name we don't curse, do magic, lie or cheat, but call to him in all adversity, pray to him, praise, and thank him.[137]

8. *Whether she believes in the one single true God: Father, Son, and Holy Spirit,*

Says confidently, yes.

9. *In whose name was she baptized at the Holy Baptism,*

Says, upon God the Father, the Son, and the Holy Spirit.

10. *Whether she knows and firmly believes that through the Holy Baptism a pact was established between God and her, and that she was taken and accepted as a child of God,*

Says, yes, without hesitation.

11. *Whether she believes that through such a baptismal pact she has attained forgiveness of sins, and that because of this if she stays consistently*

---

[136] "With a strong and grave warning." This warning does not indicate a threat of torture, but is a standard warning to tell the truth.

[137] This answer corresponds exactly to the answer in *The Small Catechism.* See p. xxxi of the Introduction.

in the proper true faith she is capable of partaking in eternal life through the merit of her Savior,

Says, yes.

12. *Whether she knows during* Anfechtungen *how to console herself with this baptismal pact with God,*

Says, yes.

13. *Whether to this time Satan has afflicted her badly with* Anfechtungen,

Says, yes, sadly as God's due.[138]

14. *When had she first noticed this seduction,*

Says, at Sangerhausen, in the council jail, before she was moved to the civic office and kept there.

15. *Whether he expected her to break her baptismal pact and to join herself to him,*

Says, absolutely yes.

16. *When, where, and how did it happen,*

Says, this past summer, fourteen days before Whitsuntide, in the jail in Sangerhausen, when she sat there in great sadness that it took such a long time before she was released, he came to her, in the form of a person of medium age, in blue clothes, and offered to her that he would soon help her get out, if she would join with him.

17. *Whether she agreed to do that,*

Says, no.

18. *How had she acted otherwise towards him, and in which way did she fight him off or turn him away,*

Says, she was terrified and fell to the ground and did not answer him at all. When she got up again, almost half an hour later, she saw nothing but fire around her, because of that she pounded her chest and begged God for mercy, as she had sinned against him.

19. *Whether her melancholy might have originated from a grave vice and evil deed that she committed,*

Says, no, instead she guesses it was because she had said out of impatience that if God and people don't want to release her, all the devils should come and release her from her suffering.

20. *Whether she was imprisoned in Sangerhausen,*

Says, yes.

21. *For what reason, and whether it didn't occur out of suspicion concerning her having committed the murder of a child,*

Says, yes.

---

[138] In the original: *leider Gottes genug.*

22. *Whether she didn't continuously fornicate carnally with a male person there,*

Says, no, she knows of no one.

23. *Who is he,*

Cessat.[139]

24. *Whether she had been pregnant,*

Says, no.

25. *If she denies this, if she hadn't appeared suspicious or was thought to be pregnant, how did it happen that she was arrested as a child-murderer,*

Says, in Sangerhausen she served as a maid with a granary official, named Siegmund Heinrich Hoffmeyer, and his housewife. His stablehand, Martin Schrade, and the maid Dorothea Bohlmann, her co-worker at that time, had reported her: that they had seen her, *Captivam*, standing on one occasion with the wheel-maker's apprentice, that they had chatted in the evening. The stablehand ran away, but the maid didn't know how to say anything true.

26. *Whether she perhaps killed or intended to kill other people's children,*

Says, no.

27. *How was she released from jail in Sangerhausen,*

Says, because they had no witnesses and found her guilty of nothing, and they also couldn't convict her of the smallest thing, she was let go.

28. *Whether she had the intention to kill Hilmar von Strombek's child,*

Says, no.

29. *On whose initiative or order was she supposed to do this,*

Says, a man came, an unfamiliar young fellow, the first time at Strombek's house, and treated her nicely, and said that she had eaten his bread and now she was his. And he told her that she should kill three people, amongst them the same Strombek's child. Thereupon he would give her enough for all of her days, especially enough money. And she should kill those for whom she felt the most hatred.

30. *What happened to her during her sleep at Hilmar von Strombek's, so that she whined and lamented so pitifully,*

Says, the Evil Enemy had been in front of the bed, she didn't know in what form because it was dark, she was supposed to do his bidding, to sleep with him.

31. *When she was weighed down with melancholy, why did she not reveal this to a pastor or a father confessor,*

Says, she didn't have the nerve to reveal it to anyone.

---

[139] "Remains silent."

--------------------------------- **FOLIO 8** ---------------------------------

[*Given Elizabeth's testimony that she had been imprisoned and tried in the town of Sangerhausen, the court here writes to the Sangerhausen officials, asking for a record of the proceedings there. Notice that the request comes with an offer of reciprocation.*]

To the honorable, farsighted and very wise mayors and council of the city of Sangerhausen, our especially gracious friends.

[*seal of the city affixed*]

Our service in friendship first, to the honorable, farsighted and very wise, especially gracious friends.

We inform the same in friendship how recently an unwed girl named Elizabeth Lorentz—whose father, according to her, supported himself with the blacksmith trade at Sangerhausen, to whence he went from here, but whose mother, Anna Triebel is still alive and supports herself there with lace making and needlework—came to be arrested and imprisoned, because at night at her employers she brought herself under suspicion with unusual whimpering, strange behavior and suspicious talk, specifically as if the Evil Enemy fiercely plagued her, and wanted to force her into inhuman intercourse at night with pinching and other strong coercion, and also wanted to force her to kill three people, those at whom she is most angry. And what is more, she let it be known that this came about because when she served as a maid in Sangerhausen with a granary official named Siegmund Heinrich Hoffmeyer, she was pointed out by his other staff, as if she had been pregnant, and therefore she was suspected of child murder. She was arrested by the honorable council there, and because her release took a long time, out of impatience she once burst out that if no one else wanted to free her, the Evil Enemy should help. Whereupon he appeared to her during custody in person. And he continued with his *Anfechtungen* in this place until her present imprisonment. We are now obliged through the authority of our office to investigate closely her way of life and character, especially because in different interrogations she made herself more and more suspicious. First, about what occurred in your municipality concerning the reported imprisonment: whether, and for what reason, it was initiated; what transpired during the *inquisition*; how she was finally released from the imprisonment. A comprehensive report is needed.

Therefore, we ask the same gentlemen herewith in friendship to give their careful report quickly concerning this—in aid of which the messenger is ordered to wait—just as we confidently expect. In like manner, we are offering and are ready to reciprocate in future cases in the aid of justice. Given under the seal of our city, the 3rd of January, *Anno* 1668.

Mayors and council of the city of Brunswick

--------------------------------- **FOLIO 8A** ---------------------------------

[*In this folio, Gese Lohrens, who had been imprisoned with Elizabeth, is questioned about Elizabeth's behavior in prison. The fact that the witness is testifying under oath with threat of penalty for perjury indicates that this is now part of formal court proceedings. Following Lohrens's testimony the court hears the testimony of the guard, Joachim Gödeke, who makes an observation about Elizabeth's behavior.*]

Incidental report, regarding the behavior of the imprisoned
The 4th of January, *Anno* 1668

Actum Brunswick in the Neustadt jail, the 4th of January, *Anno* 1668
Through the appointed officials.

Upon the order received, Gese Lohrens, Peter Soherling's housewife, who has now been released from prison, is questioned, *gravia admonitione*, because until yesterday she had sat in this jail for three weeks, whether she also heard or noticed anything from Elizabeth Lorentz, also imprisoned at that time—especially as they were both kept day and night in the warm parlor because of sudden frost. To that she gave as her consistent answer, that she never heard anything from her, nor heard talk that would be noteworthy, except only this, that the *Captiva* Lorentz, the Thursday before last, eight days ago at twelve midnight, lying on the ground on a stuffed sack, talked loudly in her sleep and said these words: "Johann, Johann, how do you have gold-yellow feathers on your hat?" and with that remained asleep. Because of that she—who was then also imprisoned and sitting not far away with the guard, Joachim, on a bench, and talking with him about other things, especially the said guard's bride—started and said: "Elizabeth, how are you doing?" At that, the said Elizabeth woke up enough so that she sat up and said: "How afraid I am." And with that lay down again.

Otherwise the witness neither saw nor heard anything more from her. Except she now adds to the talk she heard then, that the *Captiva* had been heard to laugh "hahaha" in her sleep, before she was addressed by the witness that time, and [the witness] got from her, Lorentz, as an answer, that it seemed in the dream that the witness had told her which words she had spoken in her sleep. Then the witness said that the oft-mentioned imprisoned Lorentz read diligently from a book and sang, for three days, not only in the evening and the morning, but also during the day, especially yesterday. The *Psalterium Davidis germanica lingua*[140] was still found in Lorentz's place,[141] that she was reading in it today. The witness confirms this and everything previous with a bodily oath *in continenti,*[142] *gravia declaratione perjurii ejusq. poena.*[143]

Joachim Gödeke, guard, *admonitus,* reports about the previous business. That while he stood guard during the night over the *Captiva,* Lorentz, he did not see or hear anything from her, except that the Thursday before last, eight days ago at midnight, she *geeinspraket,*[144] that is, she talked to herself in her sleep, on her bed, and because of that was she woken up by Peter Soherling's housewife. What she had said was not long. He couldn't make out anything more, except that she said something about a ribbon, he didn't hear more.

It was noticed about the *Captiva,* that during this *Examinis* she had to be in the foyer, and she sat there on the steps and cried. Also, when she was asked about that, she answered to the one court officer that she was crying because it has been so long for her, even though she was without *Anfechtung.*

FOLIO 9

[*This folio contains the letter from Christian Wadell, a member of the city council in Sangerhausen, in reply to the request from Brunswick. Attached to the letter were copies of the court documents from the trial of Elizabeth before the ducal court in Leipzig in August of 1667.*]

Presented the 14th of January, *Anno* 1668

To the well-respected, highly and well-learned, highly and very wise mayors and council of the city of Brunswick, our especially highly honored gracious gentlemen.

———

[140] "The Psalms of David in the German Language."
[141] Her jail cell.
[142] "Immediately."
[143] "With a strong statement of the severe penalty for perjury."
[144] This seems to mean that she mumbled intermittently.

To the well-respected, highly and well-learned, highly and very wise, especially highly honored gentlemen.

After offering the most willing service, I received the letter from you concerning Elizabeth Lorentz sent to the local city council. I want to report quickly to you, that the mentioned maiden was brought into custody initially at the city hall, and subsequently to our office, for the reason mentioned by you and for other reasons, which the attached copy of the judgment rendered describes further. And how through judgment and law, she was released because there was no *corpus delicti*.[145] But during her *inquisition* she varied several times, which would be too long to report. For example, that her father was not a blacksmith here at Sangerhausen, but rather a farmer at Gorsleben, which belongs to this jurisdiction, where her mother still resides. And is often sad, and worried about her bad beginning, because no admonishments have any effect on her, so that in the end she will commit an evil deed and forfeit her life because of it. Which is to be reported in reply at this time, after which I remain,

To the well-respected, highly and very wise council,

obligingly,

Christian Wadell

Sangerhausen, the 11th of January, *Anno* 1668

[*This is a copy of the judgment of the court in Leipzig, which was included with the letter from Sangerhausen.*]

Our service in friendship

With this, we, the *Kurfürstliche Schöppengericht* of Leipzig,[146] pronounce as lawful: the imprisoned Lorentz is further accused that she did violence to her mother, took the same by the head, and almost wrung her neck. Also, that she stabbed a miller, whom she encountered between Wolfenbüttel and Brunswick, who had wanted to rape her, and dragged the body into a ditch. Also, that she had let herself be impregnated by a miller's helper, gave birth to a living child, and murdered it. Further, that she wanted to stab Margrethe Meister's child. Whether she murdered the miller and her child, also that she administered a stab wound to the child of the *Meisterin*[147] and

---

[145] Literally, "body of the crime." In legal language, this means sufficient evidence of a crime.

[146] "Electoral Civic Court." This was a court of the electoral duke of Saxony. The descriptor, *Schöppengericht*, indicates that the court was comprised only of citizens, not members of the ducal administration. See Boehm (1942).

[147] "The *Meisterin*" = "the wife of Meister."

had planned and had the intention to murder it, is already confessed with many particulars reported, where she took and buried the miller's as well as the child's body. Also regarding the child of the Meisterin, *Inquisitin* actually did inflict a stab wound to it.

On the other hand, *Inquisitin* did not confess that she had insulted her mother in the reported way, nor was it proven against her; but regarding the child murder and killing of the miller, voluntarily reported by herself, no *Corpi Delicti* could be found, in spite of all diligence.

Furthermore, *Inquisitin* is not of full reason by all accounts, but rather brought forward what she reported out of sadness and despair.[148] Also she recanted afterwards and said that she had reported this in the belief that through this she could escape life. How it can be seen from the court report from Gorsleben, which can be found in *Actus*. 41, as they already pointed out before, how it was that she must be guarded. In addition, her {...} and similar has to be subject to the report of the *Medici*.[149]

And in regard to the act committed against the child of the Meisterin, taking into account her condition, it is sufficiently atoned through the time already suffered in jail. Further to the content of the *Inq. Acten*[150] sent, and to your question: the same may also not be given a further punishment. But at the same time, she owes Christian Kofferhausen a Christian apology and an explanation. And with this she is remanded to her closest friends, that they look out for her, so that in the future she may not do harm to herself or to someone else. As well she is put under care of the *Ministerio*[151] and should be carefully taught, what she can hold onto to ward off the temptation of the Evil Enemy, with which she has been bothered according to her own statement.

V. R. W.[152] in judgment.

Kurfürstliche Schöppengericht of Leipzig

————

Actum the 19th of August, 1667

Accordingly, through her apology Elizabeth Lorentz complied with the judgment, and she properly paid the stipulated fine. Therefore, she is freed

---

[148] In the original: *allen ansehen nach nicht bey vollkommen verstande, Sondern das ienige, was Sie berichtet aus schwermuth und verzweiffelung anbracht.*
[149] "Doctor."
[150] "Records of interrogation."
[151] This would have been the office of the regional church under the direction of a superintendent.
[152] We do not know to what or to whom this refers.

again with careful reminders and ordered in good faith into the custody of her mother. Done at the council office at Sangerhausen, the 19th of August.

Hendrich Appel von Lüttichen
Christian Vorkil
Martin Brückencamp[153]

----------------------------------- **FOLIO 10** -----------------------------------

[This folio contains Elizabeth's testimony concerning the skirt into which she says she sewed the seeds given to her by the Devil in exchange for her fingernail clippings. This matter would have been important because finding the seeds in the skirt would have constituted evidence of a pact with the Devil. It isn't clear exactly what happened in Wolfenbüttel or why she was there. In this folio Laurentius Gieseler, the city medical officer, makes his first appearance.]

RELATIO
Of this, which according to the Captiva Lorentz was supposed to be sewn into her grey skirt, but wasn't found in it, and what further happened at that time.
The 27th of January, *Anno* 1668

Actum in the Neustadt jail the 21st of January, *Anno* 1668
By the honorable Johann Schütze court officer, then Johann Velhagen and Otto Theune, both magistrates of the court, and Johann Pilgram the court scribe.

Accordingly, the young girl, Ilse Wachtmann, was released again on 18th *hujus*[154] from her fourteen-day imprisonment.[155] After that, the *Physicus* Dr. Gieseler[156] appeared at the jail in order to visit the recently arrested Elizabeth Lorentz and to determine her condition, as far as it falls under his office. At the same time, she was also questioned by the present court officials about one thing and another, and was reminded without threat to report her condition voluntarily and to speak the pure truth about what her situation is, and how it came about that she did not properly come forward,

---

[153] These names are scribbled and difficult to discern.
[154] "Of this [month]."
[155] As far as we can see, this girl had nothing to do with the trial of Elizabeth Lorentz.
[156] Gieseler was a physician who held the post of *Stadtphysicus*, which we would now call chief medical officer of the city. His report is in the next folio.

but beat about the bush. Upon that she repeated with little change what she had already put forward here and had reported, but amongst other things she used these words; she said: There was another hard item there. And when she was asked, what kind of item the same was, she continued voluntarily and confessed, that at his request she had to cut her fingernails and give them to him. For that he gave her something in return, which she had to sew into her skirt, at the top on the right-hand side above the pocket, which is at the barber's, who lives in Augustus Town at Wolfenbüttel.[157] Because of this, it was seen to be necessary to make this testimony known to the higher authority,[158] so that the reported skirt, which is supposed to be of white woolen cloth, could be fetched from Wolfenbüttel, inspected, searched for the things sewn in, and according to the findings could be further reported upon.

Today, *Dato* the 21st of January, the mentioned grey, or white woolen, skirt of the witness was brought directly to the jail, and so the imprisoned Lorentz was again brought for a *discours* before the assembled court officers and magistrates, the same was reminded not to despair. When the above-mentioned *Herr Physicus* arrived, as he also wanted to be present because of the things sewn in, he asked her amongst other things: 1.) Whether she had recently come here from Wolfenbüttel in the company of a young maiden, to ask a woman who can divine regarding a missing skirt; 2.) Whether she had taken something from the barber's, which she was obliged to replace. She answered yes to the first question, and related that before this she had known such a woman at Lehndorf,[159] and because that one had been away, she had gone to another woman, who lives in Gliesmerode[160] and to whom she paid 12 gulden. Then to the second question, that she had taken nothing with her, and when she is released again she wants to go to Wolfenbüttel and defend herself there. Yes, if she had stolen something, she would pay the penalty,[161] because she has a clear conscience regarding this, and she would not have left Wolfenbüttel like that, /: *insalutato Hospite Chirurgo:*/ [162] if a local woman from *Friesen Strasse*, had not encountered her there and talked loudly to her as she was walking, that

---

[157] Wolfenbüttel is about thirteen miles south of Brunswick, and was the seat of the Dukes of Brunswick-Wolfenbüttel. Augustus Town was a district of Wolfenbüttel.

[158] This would have been because, as a ducal residence, Wolfenbüttel was outside the jurisdiction of the Brunswick court.

[159] A village northwest of Brunswick.

[160] A village northeast of Brunswick.

[161] In the original: *daselbst ihren halß laßen wolte.* Literally, she "wanted to leave her neck there."

[162] "Without taking leave of her host, the surgeon." This implies that she left in great haste. Her host here was the barber, since barbers served as surgeons in the early modern period.

she was looked for in all the streets in Brunswick. Then the guard present there heard this talk, so that she was looked at closely by the musketeers, so that she didn't dare to return to the house of her master, but turned again towards Brunswick.[163] Here it was added by the court officers, that one should put all this aside, and she should be praised for standing by her good conscience. And if in this matter for which she is detained, she also has a good conscience, then she should talk trustingly. And because the doctor is present at the jail, she should remember to tell next about what she had received from Satan, and supposedly sewn into her grey skirt, and to tell whether the sewing had in truth taken place like that.

To that she said nothing. Because of that, the bailiff was ordered to bring into the room the grey skirt, which had been fetched here from Wolfenbüttel. He immediately did that, and stepped in front of her with the grey skirt, which he was holding in his hands in a clump. Then, as soon as she faced the skirt, she jumped up from the bench—on which she had been sitting with a basket, which she had standing beside her, with a fairly large ball of bleached white yarn with knitting needles sticking in it, to knit a pair of yarn gloves, as she had said—she turned her face to the wall, quickly unbuttoned her vest, turned completely white in the face, and started to shiver, especially with her left arm. Now, when she was standing there, she turned around, blanched and shivered. She was encouraged to turn back again and touch the skirt, which she didn't want to do in any way, but kept standing as before with her face towards the wall, with the statement that she couldn't look at the skirt. And when she was asked why, she didn't want to give a reason, with the statement that she didn't want to have the skirt, one should burn it, did her vest up again some but kept the blanched color the whole time. She was further urged to touch the skirt and to show in which place the thing sewed in was to be found, but she didn't want to touch the same because she had had a dream during the night, yet didn't want to say what it had been.

As the bailiff picked up the skirt again, which until now had been lying on the floor behind her, and had to show it to her so that she should state where that which had been sewn in was to be found. She remained standing with her face towards the wall, and said in a harsh voice, it was above the pocket, and reached around her body to loosen the skirt-apron a little and to air it, all the while her standing with shaking arms and hands did not diminish.

Now, during this, the bailiff was ordered to cut open the skirt in the fold above the pocket, and to search out what was sewn into it. Nothing was

---

[163] We cannot make sense of this sentence, and possibly the court could not either.

found between the lining or anywhere else, except in the pocket a small hard baking pear with a long stem, which was thrown at random into the parlor. The bailiff stepped up to the window with the skirt and had to lay a white sheet of paper under it, so that nothing should be overlooked or fall away. It was put to her that she was dealing in untruths. To that she said we probably can't see it /: *interim tremebat artus* :/[164] that he, meaning Satan, would not leave it tucked in there.

Then the bailiff reports that she had told how she had dreamed that one would have something new in two days. Asked, what that was supposed to mean, in two days, and what had she dreamt?

Says, the skirt had already been fetched yesterday, and had not been brought from Wolffenbüttel for the first time today. She was well aware of it, but was not allowed to tell. He had told her the previous night, and reprimanded her with it, that she had confessed and that the skirt was supposed to be fetched, and that she thought she would get free in this way. Only this would not happen, she was already his. She would not succeed, she would not free herself, he had already removed it from the skirt.

Regardless, she turned around again, and she sat down on the bench again, and as before she was pale and shaking. A low stool was put in front of her, and the skirt was placed on it. Upon that she was asked if it was still inside it, to which she replied consistently "No," and that it was removed, and that he had threatened that he would kill her and hang her.

Finally, she wiped her eyes once, as if starting to cry, but nothing followed, except that she burst out, and indeed apparently with great impatience and annoyance about her captivity, that one should not distress so much, one should let her go.

Then the bailiff had to carry the skirt out again, and he was ordered to carefully watch her knitting supplies during the day, and not to leave her alone day or night, even for a quarter of an hour.

--------------------------------- **FOLIO 11** ---------------------------------

[*This is the report of the physician, Laurentius Gieseler, following his visits to Elizabeth for observation. The original is a mix of German and Latin, and it was not possible to leave the Latin untranslated as we have done elsewhere.*]

The Report of Physician Laurentius Gieseler, MD

---
[164] "Meanwhile with trembling limbs."

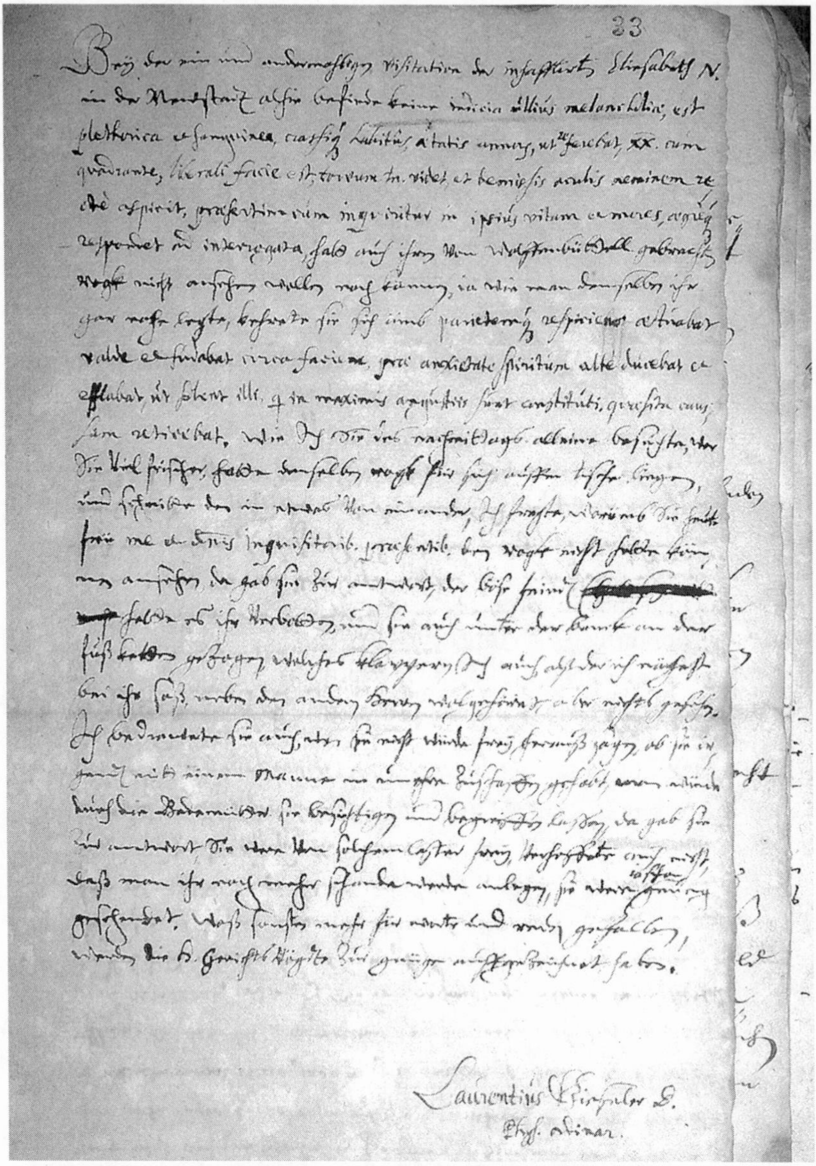

Figure 7 First page of Folio 11
Medical report of Laurentius Gieseler.

From the occasional visitation with the imprisoned Elizabeth N. here in Neustadt, I don't find signs of any form of melancholia. *Est plathonica et sanguinea*[165] with a buxom figure. Her age, as she declared, is twenty years and three months. She has a friendly facial expression. Certainly, she anticipates torture,[166] and with lowered eyes she looks at no one directly, especially when she is interrogated about her own life and her modesty. She answers such questions grudgingly. In addition, she didn't want to look at her skirt, which was brought from Wolfenbüttel, nor was she able to. Indeed, when the same was placed near her, she turned away and looked at the wall. She felt very hot, and her face perspired from fear. She breathed heavily in and out, as do those who find themselves in great peril. She gave me no answer to the question of the cause. When I visited her alone in the afternoon, she was much more fresh, had the same skirt lying in front of her on the table, and was cutting it apart into something. I asked her why, this morning in my and the investigative magistrate's presence, she was supposedly unable to look at the skirt. To that she replied, the Evil Enemy had forbidden it and he had also pulled on the leg iron under the bench, the rattling of which I clearly heard as well, as did the other officials, but I didn't see anything. I also threatened her, that, if she did not voluntarily say whether she had had dishonorable relations with any man, she would be examined and touched by a bath mother. To that she replied that she was free of such sin, also she hoped that no one would bring her any further shame, she had been dishonored often enough. Regarding further words and talk that occurred, the court magistrates will have sufficiently documented.

Dr. Laurentius Gieseler
Phys. ordinar.[167]

FOLIO 12

[In this folio, the court lists a set of questions that Elizabeth is to answer under threat of torture. Her answers are in Folio 13.]

Further *Interrogatoria*
/ 12 /

---

[165] The description *sanguinea* ("sanguine") here is a reference to the humoral medical theory. In this instance, it refers to an enthusiastic, active temperament. The word *plathonica* is unclear.
[166] The original is difficult to read, but it appears to be *torturam*.
[167] *Physicus ordinarius*: "licensed physician."

Interrogatoria

About which the *Captiva* is to be interrogated, with a prior serious reminder to confess the truth, so that one does not have to turn to stronger means:

1. Whether the Evil Enemy came to her in a physical form, when, where, and how often?
2. What he talked to her about, and
3. Whether he didn't direct her to do damage to people or animals, to whom, where, and with what?
4. Whether she obeyed him in that?
5. Whether she didn't have to bind herself to him, to be his, and to carry out his wicked will, how, where, through what, and with which words did this happen?
6. Whether he did not give her a mark /: *stigma* :/ on her body, where and in which place?
7. Whether he expected indecency from her, and did she have even intercourse with him?
8. What did he promise her in return and what did she enjoy in return for binding herself to him, did he bring her money, or did she learn magical arts in return, or what did he promise her otherwise?
9. Whether he gave her something to sew into her skirt?
10. What was it, what did it look like, and what was it supposed to be good for?
11. Whether it is still sewn into her skirt?
12. How did it happen, that recently there was nothing found in the skirt?

If she says to that, that the Evil One had taken it out of the skirt, she is to be told that this is not believable, that he is supposed to have removed it in her best interest. Because according to her report, he was ill content with her, and had said, she would be unable to get away again. So, he would not have removed the things, but, in order to further convict her, he would have left them in the skirt.

13. Whether she had to give him something in return, and what was it?
14. What did the Evil Enemy want to do with it?
15. Why, recently, when the skirt was shown to her, did she turn pale and shake so much, and did not want to look at nor touch the skirt?
16. When was the Evil Enemy with her and threatened to kill her?
17. What reason did he give for wanting to kill her?
18. Whether he still comes to her, to have indecent relations with her, and how often has it happened?

19. Whether once, while she was sitting in jail here, he did not come to her at midnight?
20. Whether she had not said overly loudly, Johann, Johann what golden yellow feathers you are wearing?
21. What had he done with her, so that she had to complain, that she was so afraid?
22. Whether he appears to her here in the jail in the form of a cat, when, how often, and to what end does he do it?
23. Whether, when the court officers showed her grey skirt, the Evil Enemy was under the bench near her and was pulling on her chain?
24. How did she know that, that it was the Evil Enemy?
25. What did he want to achieve by pulling her by the chain?
26. Why did she not report it, what was the reason for her strange behavior then?
27. How does she act towards the Evil Enemy, does she comply with his will and orders because of her pact with him, or is she able to break out of it, and how?

FOLIO 13

[*This folio records Elizabeth's answers to the questions in Folio 12. As in Folio 7, we have repeated the questions for convenience. Although she was questioned without torture, she was warned that torture could be used if her answers are not truthful.*]

The answers of Elizabeth Lorentz given without torture to the further *Interrogatoria*
The 30th *et* 31st of January, *Anno* 1668
/13 /

———

Actum in the Neustadt jail, the 30th of January, *Anno* 1668
By the honorable Johann Schütze, court officer, then Johann Velhagen and Otto Theune both magistrates of the court, and Johann Pilgram the court scribe.
Upon received orders, Elizabeth Lorentz, taken *ad Custodiam*,[168] is interrogated without torture about the further *Interrogatoria*, and testified to each as follows, which she reported after serious cautioning.

---

[168] "Into custody."

Ad. 1 *Whether the Evil Enemy came to her in a physical form, when, where, and how often,*

Says, yes, he came to her in bodily form at noon when she was sitting in the jail in Sangerhausen underneath the council chambers, only once at that place. But other than that, here in Brunswick four times at Strombek's house, but here in the current *Custodia* only once, last Wednesday, eight days ago yesterday, at night in the twelfth hour at midnight.

2. *What he talked to her about,*

Says, at Sangerhausen he talked with her and said, how she was so horribly presumptuous, and had called him, because of that he was there now. Now if she wanted to bind herself to him, he wanted to help her to get out of the jail. But because she had such a bad fright and fell to the ground, she didn't talk with him further at that time, also saw nothing more than fire, which finally went away again. Here, at Strombek's house, she was in the brew house, and because she was very frightened she sat down. Then he came to her in the form of a young man with the grey hood, and asked her why she was so sad? Yes, she should be content, he wanted to help her out of her misery, because, now that she had eaten his bread, she was his. She, however, did not answer him that time, and it happened simultaneously, that she was called by her master Strombek, and left the brew house because of that, but he stayed in it. But later, he once came in the evening, between six and seven, in front of the stove where she was lighting a fire and asked: "Did she now want to be his bride?" And he was wearing the already mentioned clothes again. But she said neither no nor yes. Because of that, he said he wanted to come to her again that same night at midnight. She was supposed to stay awake in the parlor, he wanted to talk further with her then. But the same night she had to care for the child in the bedroom because it had been acting very strangely. So, then he didn't come, and nothing came of it. But the third night after that, when she was alone in the parlor to spin her quantity of yarn, he came to her again, only now he was wearing a hat with a white feather or plumage, whereas before he was wearing a rough cap, and said it was his only desire that she should obey his will, that is, as she explained herself, to sleep with him or lie with him. But she didn't want to do that and said, no, he however said, yes. She put it off further, saying she had to think about it. To that he said and persisted further that if she had more concerns and didn't want to do it, she should promise him to kill her master Hilmar von Strombek's smallest child /: *a little son, named Johann, two years old.* :/ To that she had said yes, under the condition that she was capable of it, because she was very fond of the child, as he came to her and wanted her more than anybody else. With that he left her, in that he disappeared in front of her, even though before that he went into the parlor by the door.

She also remembers along with this, that when he came to her, he always shook her hand. His was like other people's hands but very cold. Eight days later, after he disappeared this time, he came again to her at night, around midnight, into the parlor, through the door, shook hands and kissed her, as he had done the time before. His mouth was just as cold as his hand, but his breath felt hot to her, as he stepped back again. And he said, why is it, that she always lies to him or tells him lies, that she had not killed the child? He loved her very much, but if he comes back and she has not done it, she would suffer very much. But she said, she was afraid that it would not work out well. But he replied, she should let that be his worry. If she really was incapable of killing the child, she should kill her colleague, the other maid Magdalena N. For that he would bring her a letter tomorrow or the day after. In it would be something with which she should kill the other maid. Thereupon he went to the sill by the window, and remained standing there a little while, but he started and said, now he had changed his mind. First, she should kill the child, when she had committed three murders he would bring her more than enough money, and then she should immediately leave the service of her master. Thereupon he wanted to get something of hers, and because she apologized that she had nothing, he said, if she had nothing else, she should give him the nails from her fingers. Which also happened, for she cut her nails on her left hand with a knife while Satan cut her nails on her right hand with the same knife, which is now in the jail, and is shown to her at this point, and confirmed by her with a "yes." And he took the nails and wrapped them in a piece of paper, which was lying on the windowsill. For that he gave her three black kernels in return, not as big as a pea, about the size of a *vicia* seed and with a strong smell, put them in her right hand and said, she was supposed to carry these on her and sew them into her clothes, because if she had them with her no one could do anything to her. She could plan and do whatever she wanted, even if it was not right, still no one could do anything to her. With that he urged again, that she should kill the child. But she said that she was afraid, that it would be a great misfortune. To which he answered, she should just do it, they would not think of her in connection with it, he would help her get away. She nevertheless neither agreed nor refused, so he pressed her harshly, she should decide and do it. Or else, if he returned and she had not done it, it would not go well for her. After this she had to give him her hand, and with that he left by the door. Now as she was supposed to do this but was unable to do it, she was sitting and spinning in the morning but she was full of fear. Because of this she was asked by her mistress, the *Strombeksche*, what was wrong with her, that she was sitting so sadly. Then she revealed her misfortune to her, as the same will have reported it.

But Wednesday, yesterday eight days ago, at night, after the bell rang eleven, Satan came to her in the jail through the door in black clothes and a black hat with black feathers, and without shaking hands, he sat across from her on a high stool /: *as she was still sitting on the bench, but one of the guards was lying down and sleeping, the other was sitting at the table and had a light burning, his head lying on his hand :/* and said: "Listen, how will you fare, now that you have revealed that /: *what he had talked to her about, how she was supposed to kill the child :/.*" She would not do well, and would have done better to keep her mouth shut or kept quiet and not revealed anything. But she answered nothing to that. Because of that he sat and made fun of her and laughed at her, saying further, she should watch out, when soon those with the black caps /: *not understanding whom he meant by that :/* would be sitting there, she should watch out, they would bring it about that she would have to go home without a head. He said nothing more and disappeared. But she didn't answer him at all, and only listened to his talk.

3. *Whether he didn't direct her to do damage to people or animals, to whom, where, and with what,*

Says, he ordered her to murder the child and the maid in her master Strombek's house, and then another person, whomever she wanted. He said nothing about animals and doing damage to them. She was supposed to break the neck of the Strombek child, but kill the maid as described earlier with what he wanted to bring her in a paper.

4. *Whether she obeyed him in that,*

Says no, she did not obey him, otherwise, if she had wanted to do that, she would not have revealed it to her mistress.

5. *Whether she didn't have to bind herself to him, to be his, and to carry out his wicked will, how, where, through what, and with which words did this happen,*

Says, no, she only let him have the nails, no words at all, neither good nor bad, were spoken with it, not more than she had confessed. He had kissed her, but did nothing else to her.

At this the *Captiva* is seriously reminded and carefully talked to. Yet she couldn't be moved to give a different answer. She was even resolved to await what the honorable council would be able to learn, and would learn, as she didn't know any differently, and she was in their, the gentlemen's, power.

6. *Whether he did not give her a mark /: stigma :/ on her body, where and in which place,*

Says, she doesn't know about any mark except that he squeezed her hands hard together, and hurt her with that. She could not confess more than what was the truth. When she already confesses how it was, and it were to turn out differently afterwards, she would then take responsibility for that.

7. *Whether he expected indecency from her, and did she have even intercourse with him,*

Says, while he expected indecency from her, he did so with words alone, he did not actually force her to do it. She did not have intercourse with him, nor had relations with him. So, she knows nothing about him other than that he kissed her several times, but not more than three times, squeezed her hands, and received the nails from her hands.

8. *What did he promise her in return and what did she enjoy in return for binding herself to him, did he bring her money, or did she learn magical arts in return, or what did he promise her otherwise,*

Says, she did not bind herself to him, also had not received anything from Satan to enjoy, had not learned any magical arts from him. But that he promised to give her more than enough money after she had committed the above mentioned three murders, that was true.

9. *Whether he gave her something to sew into her skirt,*

Says, yes, the three kernels.

10. *What was it, what did it look like, and what was it supposed to be good for,*

Says, she didn't know what it really was. It looked black, and its purpose was supposed to be that if she wanted to do something and bring it about, regardless no harm would come to her.

11. *Whether it is still sewn into her skirt,*

Says, no. Because he had said that it was not in it anymore, and that the skirt would be fetched.

12. *How did it happen, that recently there was nothing found in the skirt,*

Says, because he took it out and said that it happened because he was planning to free her so that she should remain in his power, and no proof would exist of the kernels.

At this she was talked to according to the instructions, that it is not believable that he should have removed it in her best interest because, according to her report, he was ill pleased with her and said she would not get away again. So, he would not have removed the things, but in order to seduce her even further would have left them in the skirt.

To that she replied, she couldn't say any differently than that he removed it, and revealed this to her the night before the skirt was fetched.

13. *Whether she had to give him something in return, and what was it,*

Says, nothing but the nails from her fingers.

14. *What did the Evil Enemy want to do with it,*

Says, he didn't say, also she didn't ask him about it.

15. *Why, recently, when the skirt was shown to her, did she turn pale and shake so much, and did not want to look at nor touch the skirt,*

Says, because he threatened her so much that, if she touched the skirt and showed in front of the authorities the place where it had been sewn in, he would wring her neck and put her in a noose. And she had seen with her eyes, even though it was hidden from the gentlemen present at that time, that when the skirt was brought into the room a small black dog came running into the room in front of the bailiff, and sat next to her on the chain with which she was secured, so that it got very heavy, and she had to forcefully hold onto it or pull it, as the gentlemen themselves had seen this pulling.

16. *When was the Evil Enemy with her and threatened to kill her,*

Says, that happened the night before the gentlemen came to the jail in the morning and the skirt was shown to her. N. had said that the skirt was in the magistrate's house.

Asked, *in which house?*

Says, it had not been named.

17. *What reason did he give for wanting to kill her,*

Says, if she would take or touch the skirt and show the place /: where it was sewn in. :/

18. *Whether he still comes to her, to have indecent relations with her, and how often has it happened,*

Says, did not expect anything of her. Also, she had not seen him since he sat across from her on the stool and made fun of her as mentioned above.

Asked, *why the guards had not heard this if it was true that he talked with her?*

Says, when he comes, he has a black thing with holes in it. He holds that in front of the light, before he talks to her, also he does not talk very loudly. The guards were asleep at the same time, and had never guarded as well as the previous night when one of them was awake the whole time. But otherwise she always had to take care of the light, when it was supposed to burn. Also, since the pastors had been to see her, she has had much peace, and hopes to get better, also hopes to turn herself to God, may it come to life or to death.

19. *Whether once, while she was sitting in jail here, he did not come to her at midnight,*

Says, the time when the skirt was fetched, or the day the skirt was brought, it was shown to her the morning after the following night.

20. *Whether she had not said overly loudly, Johann, Johann what golden yellow feathers you are wearing,*

Says, she knows nothing about this, also she can't remember having said this.

21. *What had he done with her, so that she had to complain, that she was so afraid,*

Cessat.[169]

Serio admonita.[170] Says that she often sees cats and dogs that want to bite her, she is often afraid because of that.

22. *Whether he appears to her here in the jail in the form of a cat, when, how often, and to what end does he do it,*

Says, yes. It happened several times, and she doesn't know to what end he does it, as she neither told him to do it, nor told him not to do it, but maybe he does it so that she should be afraid and not talk so much. Regardless, not only does he come when, for example, the court officer or the pastors are with her, but also when she was alone. When the one pastor came by himself recently in the afternoon, the cat sat down across from her and hissed at her, so that she couldn't contain herself out of her fear and told the pastor, who then started to pray, and took his leave afterwards.

23. *Whether, when the court officers showed her grey skirt, the Evil Enemy was under the bench near her and was pulling on her chain,*

Says, yes.

24. *How did she know that, that it was the Evil Enemy,*

Says, she could well imagine that the gentlemen didn't see the dog, and the chain got so heavy that she couldn't hold onto it, and he pulled her towards the table with it.

25. *What did he want to achieve by pulling her by the chain,*

Says, she supposes that happened in order for her to remember that she should not touch the skirt nor show the place where it was sewn in.

26. *Why did she not report it, what was the reason for her strange behavior then,*

Says, that was because of her great fear.

Asked, why had she not mentioned this fear?

Says, she wasn't allowed to. She was so afraid that she could not contain herself, because of that she also had to keep the apron string around her body open.

27. *How does she act towards the Evil Enemy, does she comply with his will and orders because of her pact with him, or is she able to break out of it, and how,*

Says, she did not make a pact with him, also she had not given him anything, except that he took the nails from her.

---

[169] "Is silent."
[170] "Gravely warned."

He hadn't brought things so far that she had to do what he wanted, it was up to her to do it or not to do it. And she gets out of it this way: that she is in doubt whether she would do it or not do it. She does not agree and also does not deny it to him. Only this time he had threatened to wring her neck if she were to touch the skirt and show the place, and that is why she was afraid, so that she didn't want to touch the skirt. While her best solace was God in heaven and prayer, yet because she had sinned so much against the dear God with her great impatience and cursing herself, she worried that God would allow him to kill her, because in her fear she is unable to pray when he appears in the above-mentioned forms.

Asked, if, against all hope, Satan should continue to come to her, with what did she want to ward him off or get away from him?

Says, according to what he wants, she would answer him with yes or no.

And because she didn't mention the Holy Book nor any sayings of comfort from it, or would use them for her freedom,[171] this is pointed out to her. She was reminded to stay with God's Holy Word and to defend herself with it, and to diligently pray and sing.

FOLIO 14

[*This is a very unusual document in a trial record. That the court recorded it as part of the official documents indicates the extent to which they made an effort to follow proper procedure.*]

The report by *Captiva* Lorentz, initiated by her, regarding the bailiff's repugnant behavior towards her.
The 6th of February *Anno* 1668

Actum Brunswick in the Neustadt jail, the 6th of February, *Anno* 1668

By the honorable Johann Schütze and the honorable Heinrich Bahre, both court officers, then Otto Theune, magistrate of the court, and Johann Pilgram, the court scribe.

Upon the received order, the above-mentioned persons of the court came to the imprisoned Elizabeth Lorentz in the Neustadt jail, because she mentioned this morning to the guard Joachim, who was attending to her,

---

[171] From the Devil.

that something else was on her heart, and the officials of the court should come to her so that she could reveal it.

She was asked what it was that was on her heart and that she wanted to reveal. At this time, it was also noticed that she was not dressed in her usual clothes and sitting as usual with fine posture on the bench. Rather she was on her bedding on the ground, and was wearing nothing other than her linens and the grey-colored suspicious skirt. At our arrival, she finally pulled herself up with half her body and sat up, breathing quickly like a patient who had much fear in her heart. She was silent during this until she was addressed for the earlier reason. Then she gave as answer that she must ask that it not be held against her. First, she wanted to make a complaint regarding her misfortune, what happened to her in the jail. That this past Tuesday evening the bailiff had been drunk, constantly used hurtful words, and said that he wanted to be rid of her in order to have a better Carnival time than he could as it was. To that she replied that it did him no harm for her to be sitting here. She countered that if God had not wanted her to be sitting here it would be better for her as well, rather than being in chains and shackles.

At that he was silent until the evening, when he started again and said that it serves them right, those who bind themselves to the Devil. She didn't respond to that until he thought again and talked about the Gospel, as was said the past Sunday, about the old Simeon who went to the temple.[172] What he said made no sense. She told him to be quiet, she knew just as well as he what he was talking about. The bailiff continued: "If you don't want to hear God's word, then you are a Devil's child." She replied again that she hadn't said that she did not want to or could not hear it, rather that he should keep quiet until he was sober, so that she could talk with him, then she would gladly hear it. At this the bailiff talked on: "How could she accuse him of being so drunk, the Devil had convinced her of this, so she couldn't hear him or listen to him." To that she said he should keep quiet. He, however, started and said, "What! I'm supposed to keep quiet for you, whore," and added, "How is it that I should keep quiet for such a foul whore and shit whore?" At that she asked where he knew this from, that she was a sin whore and a shit whore. He should prove it to her. He responded that what she had not yet done or had not yet happened, will still happen, and the executioner,[173] who had not yet been over her, soon would come behind her, before eight days are out.

---

[172] See Luke 2:25. We thank an anonymous reviewer for this reference.
[173] In early modern Germany, the executioner was also the one who carried out torture.

To that she asked whether the authorities had revealed this to him, and had ordered him to torture and frighten her, and she added that as soon as she saw one of the gentlemen walk past, she would reveal this. But to this he answered, "Did she have witnesses? He could talk as believably as she could; he wouldn't confess to it." But she replied, if there are not witnesses here, there were in heaven and she would entrust it to Him. Also at that she started to cry. The bailiff then talked and said, "Listen, now that the Devil has her in his grip, she has to cry at his bidding." But she said, "God would revenge this and make it right, as truly as she was here." He: "Where is your God? The black cat which had sat in front of the stove, on its bidding you must cry and pray to it. You dog, you are not worth as much as a dog, and not worth receiving a mouthful of bread. Such a dog! Such a foul whore!" To that she pledged to take him for a rogue until he proved to her that she was a foul whore. Then he wanted to hit her with the pitcher, or throw it at her, and asked, "Was she not a devil, did she not give him her nails, was she not an eternal devil? She had revealed it to the authorities. She can admit that she is an eternal devil and a godless person, since the pastors who she chased away with the black cat were not coming back to her. They would know best that it can't be changed; otherwise they would have come back."

Upon that she stayed silent, lay down and cried, until the guards came, to whom she reported this. Also, she had not been able to find peace after she heard that the executioner would get after her.

Note: With these words, the *Captiva* started to cry, and reported her physical condition to the *Physico* and asked about medication, complaining that she still had this fear that came upon her like a sleep so that she didn't know what was happening to her. *Dr. Physicus discessit.*[174]

Further, the *Captiva* told how she could not find peace, and asked the guards about it. In the beginning, when the guards came, the bailiff went away to his bed, but two hours later he came back into the room again and said: "I heard well how you false devils talked about me. You thunder whore!" To that the one guard replied and said: "How are we insulting you? She complained to us of how you treated her this evening. And if you did that, you haven't done right." To that the bailiff said further that this could do no harm to such a whore, because she is not only a foul whore but also a devil's whore as well. There the guard interrupted and said he should go back to bed, or if he didn't want do that, how could they be of help here? They pushed him out of the room so that he went away. She, however, collapsed, so that she didn't know what happened to her.

Otherwise she had nothing to report.

---

[174] "The physician left."

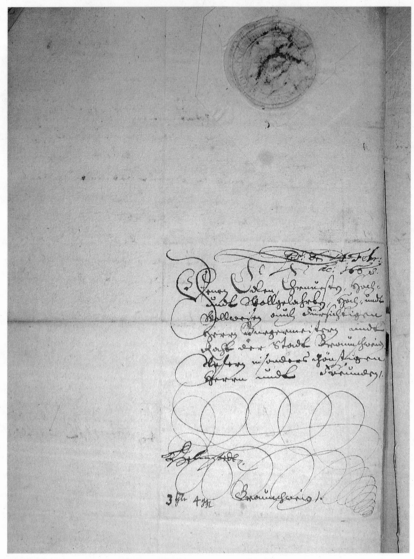

Figure 8 Cover page of Folio 15
Gutachten from the University of Helmstedt.

FOLIO 15

[*This is the* Gutachten, *or learned opinion, received by the court from the legal faculty of the University of Helmstedt. The court was not bound to follow this opinion, but such documents had great authority.*]

[*seal of the university faculty*]

Received the 14th of February, *Anno* 1668

To the noble, faithful, highly and well-learned, highly and very wise, also farsighted mayors and council of the City of Brunswick, our especially gracious gentlemen and friends,

Helmstedt

Brunswick *3 th. 4 gr.*[175]

———

Our service in friendship first, to the noble, faithful, highly and well-learned, highly and very wise, also farsighted, especially gracious gentlemen and friends.

We, *Decanus, Senior* and other doctors of the law faculty at the Duke Julius University at Helmstedt read the *Inquisitions acta* diligently with the convened *Collegio*, and considered all the circumstances sent to us, and with this returned, regarding Elizabeth Lorentz, who was arrested because of some company she kept with the Evil Enemy, and about which the gentlemen would like us to let them know and share with them our legal thoughts. Upon that we recognize as the law that, while the *Inquisitin*, partially voluntarily and partially through questioning without torture, confessed that the Evil Enemy visited her several times and talked to her, and also expected inhuman indecency from her, and desired for her to kill three people, for which he made many *promises*, and she gave him the nails from her hands, which from her left hand she cut herself, but from the right hand the Devil himself cut them. And so, it appears as if at the very least she made a *pactum tacitum*[176] with the Evil Enemy. But because she revealed her situation without pressure to the housewife of Hilmar von Strombek, her employer, at her inquiry, and there exists no accusation against her that she ever did harm to people or animals, also that when asked she recited God's Second Commandment with its interpretation. And because she believes in the one true God—Father, Son and Holy Spirit—and was also baptized in His name, through Holy Baptism a covenant between her and God was established and she was accepted and adopted as a child of God. In her answers on the 31st of December, 1667, given to the *interrogatoria* 7, 8, 9, 10, 11, *et 12*, she specifically confesses to that which people who

---

[175] "Three thaler, four groschen." Presumably, this was the charge for the *Gutachten*.
[176] "Implicit pact."

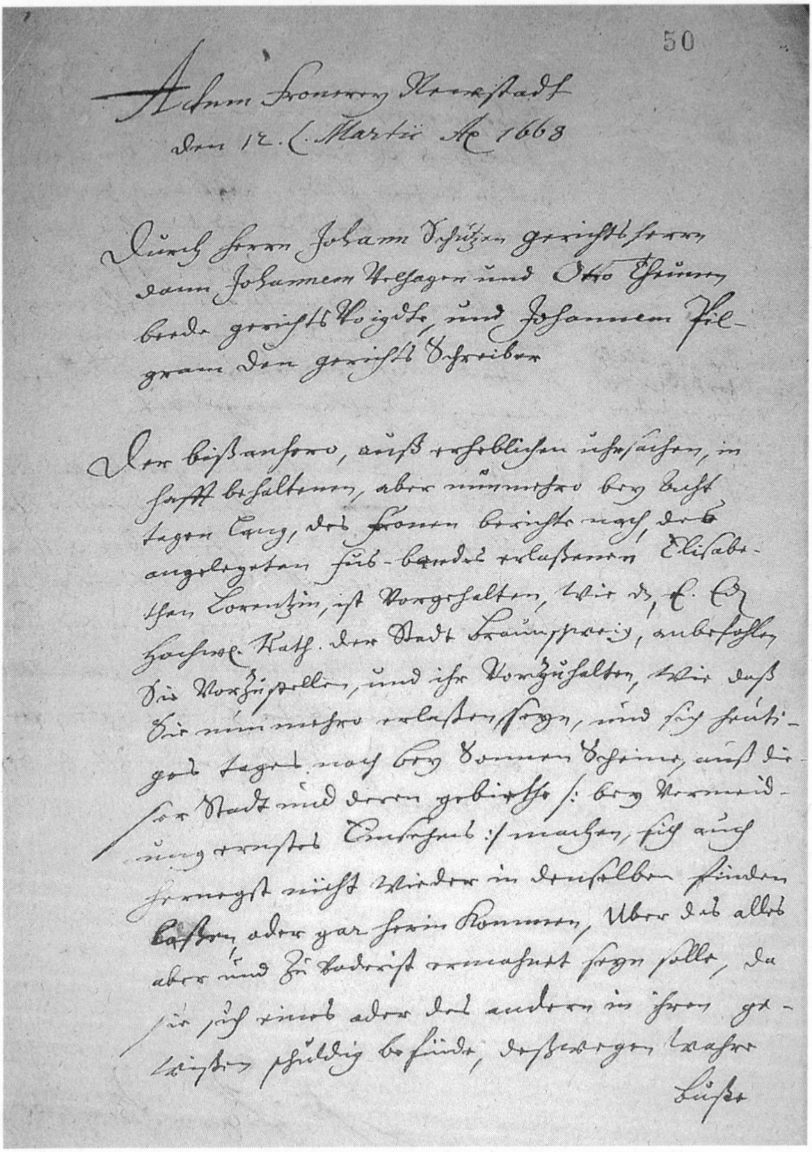

Figure 9 First page of Folio 16: Final judgment

cultivate a relationship with the Evil Enemy do not commonly do. Therefore, no torture is to be used against her, rather she should be considered as a person who is plagued by strong *Anfechtung* by the Evil Enemy, and she should not be left on her own, but should be recommended into the care of pious and God-fearing people as well as some

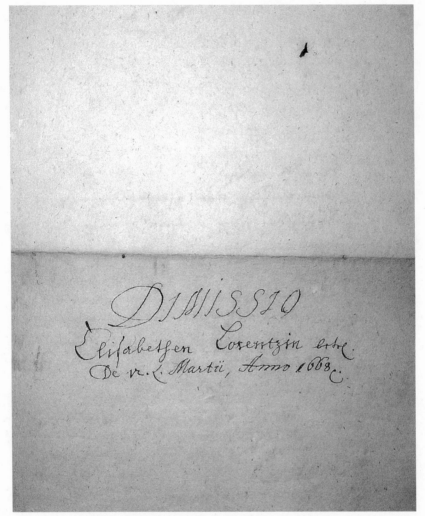

Figure 10 Cover page of Folio 16: Final judgment

from the *Ministerio* itself,[177] who can urge her and lead her to diligent prayer, singing and contemplation, as well as reading and studying the Holy Scripture at all times, until she is freed again from the temptation and *Anfechtung* of the Evil Enemy through the grace of the Almighty.

All in keeping with the law, we let this be attested by the seal of our faculty. Executed in Helmstedt, the 11th of February, *Anno* 1668.

Decanus Senior and other *Doctores* of the faculty of law here.

---

[177] See the recommendation of the court in Sangerhausen in Folio 9.

--------------------------------- **FOLIO 16** ---------------------------------

[*This is the final judgment of the court. After this event, Elizabeth Lorentz disappeared from recorded history.*]

DISMISSIO
regarding Elizabeth Lorentz
the 12th of March, *Anno* 1668

Actum in the Neustadt jail, the 12th of March, *Anno* 1668
By the honorable Johann Schütze, court officer, then Johann Velhagen and Otto Theune, both magistrates of the court, and Johann Pilgram, the court scribe.

It is put to Elizabeth Lorentz, for good reason imprisoned, but for eight days now freed of the leg-iron, according to the bailiff's report, that the honorable most worthy Council of the City of Brunswick, is ordered to bring her forward and put to her that she is now released and today, while the sun is still shining, must leave the town and its jurisdiction /: *in order to avoid serious consequences* :/, also not to let herself be found in the same again, or even enter it. But more than anything and primarily she should be reminded to do true penance, as she finds her conscience guilty of one thing and another.

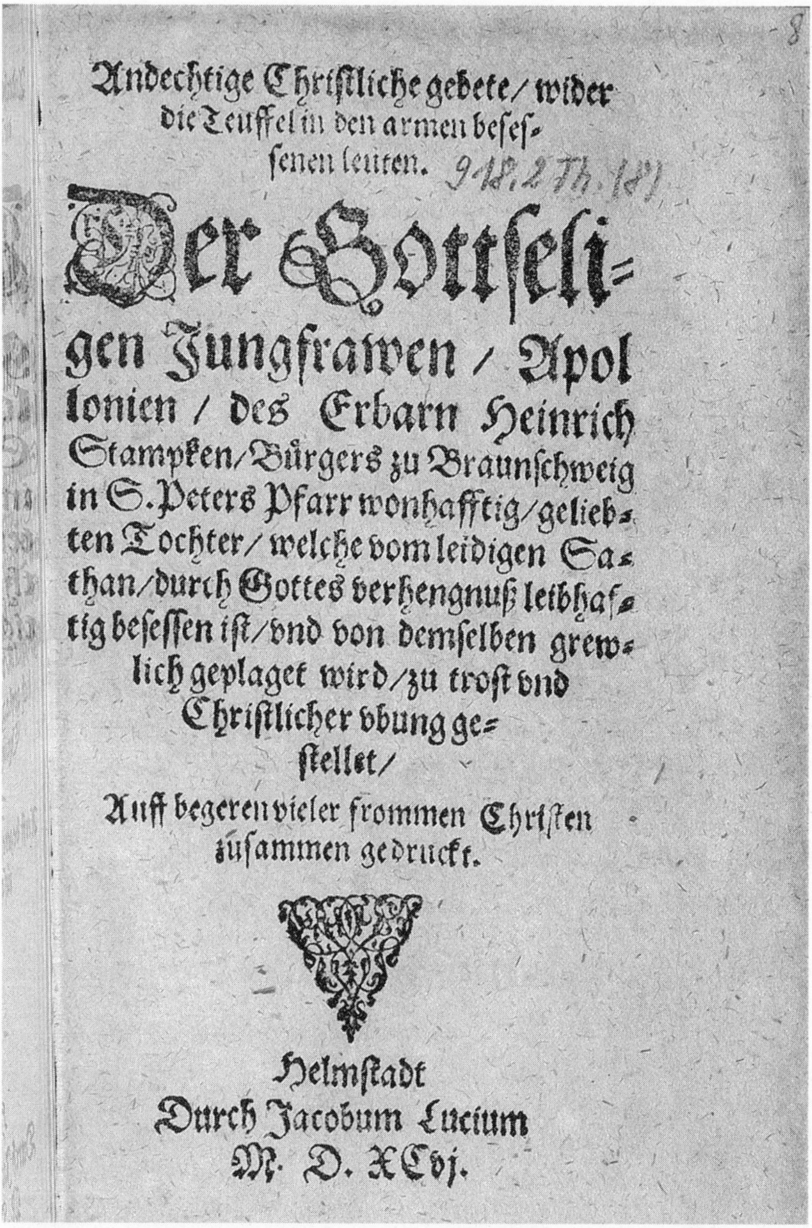

Andechtige Chriſtliche gebete/ wider die Teuffel in den armen beſeſſenen leuten.

Der Gottſeligen Jungfrawen / Apollonien / des Erbarn Heinrich Stampken/Bürgers zu Braunſchweig in S.Peters Pfarr wonhafftig/geliebten Tochter/ welche vom leidigen Sathan/durch Gottes verhengnuß leibhafftig beſeſſen iſt/vnd von demſelben grewlich geplaget wird/zu troſt vnd Chriſtlicher vbung geſtellet/

Auff begeren vieler frommen Chriſten zuſammen gedruckt.

Helmſtadt Durch Jacobum Lucium M. D. XCvj.

Figure 11 Melchior Neukirch, *Devout Christian Prayers against the Devils*, 1596 (title page)

Figure 12   Church of St. Peter, Brunswick
The church where Appolonia Stampke was a member of the congregation
and Melchior Neukirch was the pastor in 1596, as it appears today.

Appendix

Melchior Neukirch
*Devout Christian Prayers against the Devils
in the Poor Possessed People*
Helmstedt: Jacob Lucius, 1596
Signature:
A1-B5
D1-D3

[Melchior Neukirch (1540–1597) was pastor of the Church of St. Peter in Brunswick. His father was educated in Wittenberg at the outset of the Reformation, and was a Lutheran pastor of the Church of St. Andreas in Brunswick. Neukirch was educated in Rostock, and first held the position of rector in Husum. In the year of his father's death in 1566, Neukirch returned to Brunswick to take up an office in the school of St. Catherine and St. Aegidius. In 1571, he became pastor of St. Peter, a position he held until his death of the plague. His most well-known publication is a verse dramatization of the martyrdom of St. Steven in Acts 6–7. He published a number of other books, both in Latin and German. Among them is Neukirch (1596b), a set of sermons on the death and resurrection of Lazarus in John 11:1–44. In this work, he used the story of Lazarus and his sisters to make the point that we must always trust in God, even unto death itself. This view reflects the attitude he adopts in treating Appolonia.

Translated here is the preface to a collection of prayers for those suffering from demonic possession. The preface describes the possession of Appolonia Stampke. The prayers were written by Neukirch and three superintendents of

the Brunswick church: Joachim Mörlin, Martin Chemnitz, and Lucas Mar-
tini. The latter was in office during Neukirch's tenure at St. Peter.]

Devout Christian prayers against the devils in the poor
possessed people, concerning the pious maiden, Apollonia,
beloved daughter of the honorable Heinrich Stampke,
citizen of Brunswick living in the parish of St. Peter,
who, through God's decree, is bodilypossessed by the
wretched Satan, and is horribly tortured by the same,
are given for solace and Christian practice.

Helmstedt
Jacob Lucius
M.D. XCVI

———

PREFACE
To my dear flock and Christian congregation of the Church of St. Peter in
the worthy town of Brunswick.

As Your Dear Lordship knows, the almighty God, according to his
secret and hidden council and fatherly will, inflicted[178] upon a person of
this community—a devout and pious maiden with a simple Christian
heart, who behaved from childhood onward modestly, honestly, and as a
good Christian; who learned her catechism carefully since childhood and
loved the same in her prayer, including the evening and morning benediction; who diligently attended the sermons; who also always showed great
devotion to the precious communion of the Lord and the holy absolution—that for roughly three quarters of a year she should fall into weak-
ness of body as well as despondency, and for a time had severe internal
Anfechtung.[179] In the end she exhibited strange behavior and speech, from
which her parents and friends, who are also pious, devout people, formed
all sorts of thoughts, and they sent a messenger to me, as their father confessor and spiritual advisor, and complained to me about this misery.

But then I didn't want to fall straightaway into the idea (which isn't
proper) that one should immediately say and believe that the Devil was
there in person. For sometimes it happens with severe illness of the head
or another pestilence that one notices in the patient's strange gestures and

---

[178] In the original: *verhänget*.
[179] For the meaning of *Anfechtung*, see the Introduction, pp. xxxviii–xl.

talk, but nevertheless it turns out afterwards that it was only confusion in the head and disorder of reason. One should observe it for a while to see how it develops further, and, in the meantime, people who might come should not be permitted to talk a lot about other things[180] and lead the sick person further into sad thoughts, but rather to talk her out of those things as far as possible, until it finally becomes apparent what, through God's decree,[181] might be present. And as it happened, soon afterwards, the maiden desired that the Lord's sacrament might be given to her, and I had previously had various conversations with her, so while I heard several things that weren't right, nevertheless I made great effort to lift those thoughts as much as possible from her heart. Whereupon she appeared quite peaceful, did her confession, and received holy absolution. The following day I came back to her again and administered to her the sacrament of communion, and then something must have happened, for it transpired that without serious obstacles she performed and completed her Christian endeavor through God's help and mercy.

But as soon as I left her she immediately burst out with much vehemence in words and gestures, and yet afterwards she again turned a bit quieter, until after several days she became ever worse. Then I was once again summoned to her, and from then on, I visited her diligently. I consoled her with God's word and diligently reminded her to defend herself from the *Anfechtung* with verses from Scripture and her prayers. Yet the longer it lasted the more it became evident what a calamity was at hand. That is why I brought this wretched, miserable adversity to our *colloquio*[182] and to the Superintendent, and I asked my fellow brothers to also visit the poor, sad person, and to console her with God's word in addition to me, and to talk her towards peace. Which they did with all diligence; they also conscientiously kept her in all the prayers in their sermons. As the misery kept increasing and the Devil showed himself more horribly from day to day, they visited her even more assiduously. And then, as was particularly proper for me as her father confessor and pastor, I prayed daily with her at her sick bed, and diligently put before her the finest verses of consolation from Scripture, which helped her especially. And when the Evil Enemy finally let himself be openly heard and perceived with mocking and blasphemous speech, with God's word I threatened and subdued him.

At that time, she was also visited daily by her friends and other pious Christians who also prayed with her and consoled her with God's word. Finally, she implored me several times again, saying that she would like

---

[180] Presumably, the Devil.
[181] In the original: *Verhängnus*.
[182] This would refer to a meeting of the Brunswick pastors.

again to be given absolution and communion of the Lord. Here I have to confess that at this time I almost had concerns about performing immediately what she desired at that time, because the Evil Enemy, when he noticed what the maiden was planning, showed himself very ferociously.

Yet nevertheless I also did not want to deny the sad heart her Christian desire, nor hold her back for too long. I initially beseeched her for eight days to pray diligently. Also, I beseeched the whole Christian community, which gathered at that time at St. Catherine's for the catechism sermon, to diligently beg daily on her behalf that God Almighty might support her through his mercy in her Christian endeavor, and that he might forbid the Devil to hinder her. Also, in the meantime I reminded her how to conduct herself properly and prepare for the receiving of absolution and communion. And finally, after that, I let her make her confession on her sick bed in her father's house on St. Aegidius's Day in the presence of many other pious Christians as well as the Superintendent and all the ministers. Then, because the dear God showed great mercy, I gave her absolution and administered communion to her so that even though Satan himself fought against it horribly and tried to prevent this Christian work, nevertheless he was incapable of it; rather through God's mercy, to whom we called faithfully in this, he was forced to let everything occur.

After this time, I actually first heard from her what the origin of her great misfortune was, and what had caused it in the beginning. As follows: she had been somewhere where someone out of violent anger had cursed her to the Devil. After that she soon felt pain and fear in her heart, so that she fell to the ground and bemoaned this curse. Yet afterwards as it calmed down again, so that she didn't notice anything unusual anymore, she hoped that there would be no peril to her, and she was more or less at peace with this, although she complained of it to her parents. And from then on, she often noticed strange thoughts, so that it entered her mind that she was not God's child and could not receive God's mercy, and also that she did not belong among God's children and the elect. She was often puzzled by that, and wondered from where such thoughts might come to her. And when they nearly overwhelmed her, she threw herself into prayer and fended them off in that way. Until finally, after about a year had passed, she was walking alone in the dark, in her father's yard. While she didn't see anything, she heard a loud racket on the roof that frightened her a great deal. She ran to the house, rushing for the parlor, but ended up in the cellar. However, she drew herself together and came back out, and remained lying in front of the door, and from this shock she fell into a swoon and contracted a fever, so that in her dreams and also in waking, she often became frightened. At first, she thought that she was unwell, until it finally came about that the Devil let it be known that he was present in her. For a long time, she fought him off with prayer and verses of Scripture, until it finally became too much, and she had to tell of it and complain about it to her parents, who then further reported it to me as their pastor.

When she gave me this report, as I said, after she had received communion for a second time and was comforted further by me and reminded to be patient, soon after that God granted her mercy, in that, while before she had had to lie in bed continuously for almost half a year and could never leave it, on the following Sunday (just in the moment that we did our prayer for her) she suddenly got such strength and vigor that she got up from her sick bed and walked about the house. She cheerfully greeted her father and mother when they came home from church. She sat down at the table with them, ate and drank, and immediately let me know about this. And when I visited her the following Monday, she said that if it was acceptable to me she would come to my church on Wednesday to attend my sermon, which she also did. And from that day on she never missed any of my sermons, but rather she came to my church every Sunday, Monday, and Wednesday, diligently and devoutly praying. Which, from that day on, I did after all my sermons on Sundays and workdays, because I then saw that not solely my dear pastoral children drew joy from this, and always urged me not to be discouraged in my efforts, but to remain steadfast in my prayers. For not only does your lordship faithfully support me with prayer and song, but also the people from the entire town often find their way here and diligently help in prayer with great devotion. It also heartens me that I earnestly care for my appointed pastoral child, despite the wicked enemy's deliberate sacrilege and blasphemy and his disdain of our prayer and Christian practice, and despite the huge, heavy effort and reluctance that this action entails, as well as those who can be found who, with the mockery that they derive from this, almost make me disinclined to dare to pull her back with prayer and God's help from the mouth of the hellhound. Nevertheless, to this day I remain and persevere through God's mercy with the work that I began. And after all my sermons I took the possessed person and introduced her to the congregation, so that each Christian could see and observe her immense suffering and misery, could care for her, and diligently beg God on her behalf and call to him, that God may comfort her in her heavy burden, may give her patience, that for God's grace, she may be kept in the true faith and real confidence, and to fight off all the Devil's *Anfechtungen*, and when his time comes to drive him from this temple of the Holy Spirit, which pleases him, and to order him to the depths of hell.

At the same time, I caution the raw, wild, godless people that they shouldn't be found at this pitiful spectacle out of curiosity, but rather they should observe what God reveals through this pious person, and how they should use it and better themselves through it. Then further I hold the Devil to God's judgment, which stands above him and upon which the hellish fire is readied for him in the place where he belongs. He has no power over Christians, and so he should leave this person, as a little lamb of the Lord Jesus, and depart from her. With the entire community, I call to God over him and against him; I remind Him of His power and strength against His declared enemy, and that He may take up judgment and drive him from this temple.

My Lord Christ, as the First Shepherd, who redeemed her with his blood, and ripped her out of the throat of the hellish wolf, ordered that I should care for the same, as for all my appointed pastoral children, that they might not become of the Devil. Therefore, I commanded the Devil through the power of my office, conferred on me by God and through which I am able to order the Devil, to leave this person, my pastoral child, untormented and not to hinder her, so that she might show her faith and her confession bravely in the face of God and the Christian community.

But because the Devil twisted and fought back, and wanted to prevent this, the poor person often stopped for a long time when she had the words on her tongue. Her lips moved and she dearly wanted to pronounce the prayer, but she was often prevented by the Devil for a long time. Until finally against his will he has to oblige her, which really should be a great joy and solace to all pious Christians, when they see that God, as the mightiest Prince of this world, is stronger. Which is also why one has to continue with prayer and not tire, until God the Almighty, at the time when He desires and at the hour that He ordained for it, will come, will show his merciful help and salvation for this miserable person, and free her from the great violence and attacks of Satan himself, and banish him once again into the depths of hell.

But for the arrogant and the godless, this sad, miserable spectacle should serve to lead them to fear God, to avoid sin, repent, and walk in a new obedience to their Heavenly Father as his good children, so that they will not forever remain in the Devil's power and control, but rather let themselves be governed by the Holy Spirit and practice prayer and Christian devotion. That is also why litanies and other Christian psalms and pious songs are sung in between the little prayers, and beautiful consoling verses from the Word of God and the pious psalms of David are read to the person and briefly explained, and the use of the same is shown and taught to her. And finally, the whole *actus* is brought to an end with the beautiful comforting song, "Christ, you who are the bright day etc.,"[183] after which, in the end, I bless the community and remind them to diligently pray, in their homes as well, for this sad person and also for themselves. After that I excuse the congregation and say the benediction over this person, reminding her to be patient and to wait for the hour of God, when God in the end will surely rescue her from her heavy burden and mercifully free her.

I have so far adhered to this Christian proceeding with this poor, miserable, sad person, until she again, this past twenty-first Sunday after *Trinitatis*,[184] through her heartfelt desire and Christian preparation, brought herself to the Table of the Lord. Just as I had prepared her the whole previous week, and particularly the Friday before, I led her in my church through the entire catechism in the presence of several pious matrons. And because she herself recited each single piece of the catechism clearly and intelligibly by herself, regardless of how much the Devil had wanted to hinder and prevent her, I instructed her in the proper use of such teachings: how she should recognize and look upon her sins according to the Law, that through the wages of sin we all belong under the power of the Devil, and how eternal damnation must befall us; how one should take solace through faith, that God, the Heavenly father, out of beautiful love and mercy, gave his only Son to the world, and because of us, He entered into the Law and fulfilled it in our place and freed us from the curse of the Law, obtained and earned eternal life and salvation; how the Holy Spirit awakens, strengthens, and preserves such faith in us through the Word and the Holy Sacraments for forgiveness of sin and eternal life; how one should make such solace one's own and use it through daily prayer, and to seal and assure the same through the use of the Holy Sacraments and absolution.

Whereupon I further had her come the following Saturday to the church, and before I listened to the confessions of my other pastoral children, I took her into the church first, let her do her confession and recite other fine prayers, and upon that I absolved her from her sins and freed her. She received the absolution in the presence of a worthy congregation with great joy. But against this the Devil showed himself angrily and grimly, yet nonetheless he had to let it happen. Thereupon, for comfort and finality, I briefly explained the 32nd Psalm of David, and I gave it to her to take home so that she could take further solace for her heart from it, and to console herself again through the absolution received and the forgiveness of her sins.

---

[183] *Christe, du bist der helle Tag.* Erasmus Alber (c. 1500–1553).
[184] Trinity Sunday, the first Sunday after Pentecost.

The following Sunday, after the sermon had ended, she was to be found in the choir of the church with other recipients of the communion and listened with devotion to the service for the communion. And although the Devil really wanted to interrupt and be heard with much sacrilege and malice, through God's mercy she received the communion unimpeded, over which the whole church rejoiced and thanked God for this mercy.

But from that day on the poor person was plagued horribly by the Devil, for through her the Devil created great commotion in the church during the sermons, with shouting, blasphemy, and mocking of God's word and prayer. It is horrible and wrenching to watch it, right to this hour, today. From this the poor person gets very weak, tired and without strength, and is hindered by the Devil so that she now has trouble enjoying earthly food and drink. And the most burdensome and dangerous thing is that, while she had been able to resist the Devil strongly in her heart and fight with him and comfort herself with God's word, now the wretched Satan dares to rip this solace from her heart and tortures her with gruesome, horrible *Anfechtungen*. He suggests to her that she should kill herself, or yield and grant him a little bit of power; soon he would help her out of this. This she bemoans to me with tears every day and to those who are around her. Therefore, now a great effort is necessary, to remain in prayer and to call on God the Almighty even more diligently for Him to ward off this endeavor of the Devil, and to strengthen the saddened heart and to keep it in the true faith. Now many pious Christians congregate and find their way daily to this prayer, including the Superintendent and other pastors, who are now present personally to faithfully help pray and also to remind the congregation to pray diligently. For we don't want to doubt that God the almighty and merciful Father will finally and surely listen to our prayer, and to the prayer of the poor person, which she does with great devotion for the honor of His name.

In order that the whole community can pray with us and have at hand the Christian prayers that we preachers and the possessed person recite, at the many requests of a multitude of pious Christians, I have printed together these same devotional prayers, which we preachers recite for the possessed person and direct against the Devil, and which we ourselves recite from a devout heart and a zealous spirit, so that I often find my joy in it and through which I overcome the great effort to which this action brings me.

[Such prayers] were also brought together that were used before this time by the two superintendents, in blessed memory, Doctor Joachim Mör-lin and Doctor Martin Chemnitz, at a time during which the same misfortune also occurred in this community through God's decree *Anno* 1556 and 1574. And also [those which] were in this present case directed by the current Superintendent Master Lucas Martini towards this person, also [those which], as the sad person's father confessor and spiritual advisor, I prescribed for her solace and for Christian devotion, in addition to noting several comforting passages from the Holy Bible. When I visited this person at her sick bed and when she later came to my house and the church, I put these before her and showed her, and also explained them briefly to her. And I do not doubt that this will please pious Christians, who will also be consoled through this in their suffering and concerns, which God sends to everyone according to His fatherly will and His pleasure. May the Almighty God and Father of our Dear Lord and Savior Jesus Christ bring it about that we use this Christian lesson fruitfully for instruction, remembrance, warning, and comfort, and that this miserable, pitiful spectacle may be used for our solace, not as a miraculous wonder[185] but as a mirror of the rage against sin, in order to avert all certitude and impenitence. And may the presence of the Holy Spirit in this person be used for solace, so that the Holy Spirit is also alive and strong in our hearts, that we all may overcome in this way the *Anfechtungen* of the wretched Devil, which God the Almighty Father, for the sake of His dear Son, our Lord and Savior Jesus Christ, through the spirit of His dear Holy Angels, mercifully grants us, and protect us from the Devil and all his power and cunning.

Datum Brunswick, St. Martin's Day in the year of our Lord 1596.

Melchior Neukirch,

Pastor of the Church of St. Peter in the city of Brunswick

———

DEVOUT CHRISTIAN PRAYERS AGAINST THE DEVILS IN THE POOR POSSESSED PEOPLE

[Included in the following are only the prayers by Neukirch himself. The prayers by Martin Chemnitz, Lucas Martini, and Joachim Mörlin are not included. The prayers are translated literally, without attempt to replicate the rhyme and rhythm of the originals.]

Many Christian and devout little prayers for the possessed maiden, composed by her pastor for her solace, to resist the Devils and to seek
God's help with them.
Which she has also taken into herself.
Which she has used for herself at home, and publicly in the church as testament to her faith and trust in God, always spoken with great devotion.

---

[185] In the original: *fürwitz*, which in this context probably implied curiosity.

The First

I hope and I am completely sure
That God is my friend in Christ,
Even if he weighs me down with burden,
And jolts me now and again.

Yet still he will never hate me,
Nor will he ever leave me.
He will also vex the hellish Devil.
I will still eternally find joy
With all the holy angels,
And with God's elect.
And with the mercy and compassion
Of God through all eternity,
Through Jesus Christ, Son of God,
Who is my Savior and Redeemer.
Amen

A Second

Oh, Son of God, Lord Jesus Christ,
Who has come to earth
To destroy the Devil's work.
Oh Lord, turn now also to me
In my wailing and misery.
Come to help me quickly and soon.

Destroy the Evil Enemy's might,
Power, defiance, outrage, deceit, and pomp,
By which through God's command
He plagues me and causes me pain.
Control his great tyranny,
Which he practices on me in so many ways.
And comfort me in this distress, dear God,
And my great burden, my Lord.
And let your word be to my heart
An eternal solace and joy,
So that in this great misery
I do not despair in my heart.
But rather trust in your great strength,
Promised to me through your word,

That you will stand with your aid
By your dear children
When they are in distress and fear,
When no one else can be of help.
Oh Lord, in this great distress
That now confronts me,
Now that the wretched Evil Enemy
Through your will fiercely plagues me
In my body, and would dearly love
To turn my heart away from you.

Don't leave me, my Lord and God
In this great heavy distress.
The Devil exerts great force,
And torments me horribly in many ways.
He takes hold of me in all my limbs
Tears at me, and causes me great pain.
Oh Lord, release me from this anguish.
Preserve my body and soul.

The Enemy is ferocious and strong
Yet you are stronger still.
He who is Lord of all this world,
You have overcome him and felled him,
Taken from him his armor,
With which otherwise he would have deceived.
With your verses, you have
Trampled and crushed him.
His castle, Hell, destroyed,
And in triumph led him away.
And, with chains of darkness,
You have trussed him and pushed him out
Into the eternal slough of hellish embers.
Oh Lord, take me into your care
And protect me from the Dog of Hell.
Let the blissful hour arrive
In which, when it pleases you,
You save me from his great might.
Amen

A Third

When we are in the greatest distress
And know not where to turn,
We have in the beginning and end,
In our hearts, still this advice:
That to you, Oh faithful God,
We all turn in our distress,
And lift our eyes and heart
To you in this misery and pain.
There too in this time
When all sorrow lies in me,
I come to you in firm faith.
Oh highest God, be merciful to me,
Rule and govern all my affairs,
Deliver me from all adversity,
So that everything that we do
Is to bring praise and honor to you.
Oh Lord, you have promised us
We should ask without despair,
And call upon you in distress.
Then you will stand by us faithfully,
And listen to us mercifully,
That we shall praise you afterwards.
This your promise we embrace,
And stay with you in faith.

Help me through your Son, Jesus Christ,
Who is the proper help in need.
Console me in my great misery,
Strengthen my faith until my end.
Take pity on all your children
Who are beside me in affliction.
Take away all of our sadness,
Turn it into eternal joy,
So we will praise you,
And glorify you on the highest throne.
Oh stay by me, Lord Jesus Christ,
While great distress is at hand.
Don't let the bright light, your Holy Word,
Go out in me.

In this great danger,
Give me faith and endurance,
That I will keep your Word and Sacrament
Pure until the end.
Amen

A Fourth

Lord Jesus Christ, Son of God,
My savior, mediator, and patron,
I, poor sinner, come to you.
While you speak, it all comes to me:
"All those who stand in fear and distress,
I will save you from sin and death.

I will be your solace and support,
Through your God, my Father,
I will give you through my word and spirit,
Righteousness and eternal life."
I believe, Lord, in your word and in you.
You [are] joy and solace in my heart.
If you leave me I stand bereft.
Therefore, I beg of you through your great benevolence,
Through your sacrifice and precious blood,
Which will wash away all my sins,
Remember me, oh son of God,
In your dear Father's throne.
In the Devil's sieve[186] now I sit,
If you leave me I shall perish.
Do not leave me in this distress,
Relieve all my suffering,
Stand by me with love and faith.
In you alone is rest and peace.
You are my rock, my shield and treasure.
In your father's house, speak for me.
You are the highest priest immaculate,
Put out a prayer for me
When my faith sinks and falters
And my great sins plague me.

---

[186] In old German, this can also refer to a net for catching fish or birds.

No solace will come to my heart,
And it is panicked from fear.
All creatures are against me.
The Devil and death strive
To separate me, a poor child, from you.
Stand by me, my God and Lord,
When body and soul are parted.
So, sprinkle me, Lord, with your blood.
The people have no part in me,
On you alone rests all my salvation.
A poor heart is aching with remorse,
Sprinkled with your precious blood.
Such sacrifice pleases God alone.
Let my soul be commanded to you.
Grant me, Lord, a blessed end,
Take my spirit in your hand,
Preserve your poor Christendom,
And keep it in peace and pure faith.
Amen

Works Cited

Almond, Philip C. 2014. *The Devil: A New Biography*. Ithaca, NY: Cornell University Press.

Althaus, Paul. 1966. *The Theology of Martin Luther*. Minneapolis: Fortress Press.

Augustine of Hippo. 1958. *On Christian Doctrine*. Translated by D.W. Robertson Jr. New York: MacMillan Press.

Bailey, Michael D. 2003. *Battling Demons: Witchcraft, Heresy, and Reform in the Late Middle Ages*. University Park, PA: Pennsylvania State University Press.

Balduin, Friedrich. 1628. *Tractatus luculentus, posthumus, toti rei publicae Christianae utilissimus, de materia rarissime antehac enucleata, casibus nimirum conscientiae*. Wittenberg: Paul Hedwig.

Baron, Frank. 1978. *Doctor Faustus from History to Legend*. Humanistische Bibliothek 1: 27. Munich: Wilhelm Fink.

Baron, Frank. 1992. *Faustus on Trial: The Origin of Johann Spies's "Historia" in an Age of Witch Hunting*. Frühe Neuzeit 9. Tübingen: Max Niemeyer.

Baron, Frank. 2009. *Hermann Witekinds "Christlich Bedencken" und die Entstehung des Faustbuchs von 1587. In Verbindung mit einer krit. Edition des Textes von 1585 von Benedikt Sommer*. Studium Litterarum: Studien und Texte zur deutschen Literaturgeschichte. Berlin: Weidler.

Bast, Robert James. 1997. *Honor Your Fathers: Catechisms and the Emergence of a Patriarchal Ideology in Germany, 1400–1600*. Leiden: Brill.

Die berühmte braunschweiger Stadt- und Kleiderordnung von 1579: Reprint der Originalausgabe. 1978. Braunschweig: Stadtkirchenverband Braunschweig.

Biller, Peter, and Alastair J. Minnis, eds. 1998. *Handling Sin: Confession in the Middle Ages*. York Studies in Medieval Theology 2. York: York Medieval Press.

Blumenfeld-Kosinski, Renate. 2010. "The Strange Case of Ermine de Reims (c. 1347–1396): A Medieval Woman between Demons and Saints." *Speculum* 85 (2): 321–56.

Blumenfeld-Kosinski, Renate. 2015. *The Strange Case of Ermine de Reims: A Medieval Woman between Demons and Saints*. The Middle Ages Series. Philadelphia: University of Pennsylvania Press.

Bode, Gerhard. 2008. "Instruction of the Christian Faith by Lutherans after Luther." In *Lutheran Ecclesiastical Culture, 1550–1675*, edited by Robert Kolb, 159–204. Leiden: Brill.

Bodin, Jean. 2001. *On the Demon-Mania of Witches*. Translated by Randy A. Scott. Renaissance and Reformation Texts in Translation. Toronto: Centre for Reformation and Renaissance Studies.

Boehm, Ernst. 1942. "Der Schöppenstuhl zu Leipzig und der sächsische Inquisittionsprozeß im Barokzeitalter." *Zeitschrift Für Die Gesamte Strafrechtswissenschaft* 61 (1): 371–410.

Bossy, John. 1983. "The Mass as a Social Institution 1200–1700." *Past and Present* 100 (August): 29–61.

Bossy, John. 1985. *Christianity in the West, 1400–1700*. Oxford: Oxford University Press.

Bossy, John. 1988. "Moral Arithmetic: Seven Sins into Ten Commandments." In *Conscience and Casuistry in Early Modern Europe*, edited by Edmund Leites, 214–34. Cambridge: Cambridge University Press.

Brown, Phyllis R., Linda A. McMillin, and Katharina Wilson, eds. 2004. *Hrotsvit of Gandersheim: Contexts, Identities, Affinities, and Performances*. Toronto: University of Toronto Press.

Brown, Phyllis R., and Stephen L. Wailes, eds. 2013. *A Companion to Hrotsvit of Gandersheim (fl. 960): Contextual and Interpretive Approaches*. Brill's Companions to the Christian Tradition 34. Leiden: Brill.

Bugenhagen, Johannes. 1912. *Johannes Bugenhagens braunschweiger Kirchenordnung 1528*. Edited by Hans Lietzmann. Bonn: Marcus & Weber.

Caciola, Nancy. 2000. "Mystics, Demoniacs, and the Physiology of Spirit Possession in Medieval Europe." *Comparative Studies in Society and History* 42 (2): 268–306.

Caciola, Nancy. 2003. *Discerning Spirits: Divine and Demonic Possession in the Middle Ages*. Conjunctions of Religion and Power in the Medieval Past. Ithaca and London: Cornell University Press.

Cameron, Euan. 2010. *Enchanted Europe: Superstition, Reason, and Religion, 1250–1750*. Oxford: Oxford University Press.

Cantor, Norman F. 2001. *In the Wake of the Plague: The Black Death and the World It Made*. New York: Simon and Schuster.

Christman, Robert. 2008. "The Pulpit and the Pew: Shaping Popular Piety in the Late Reformation." In *Lutheran Ecclesiastical Culture, 1550–1675*, edited by Robert Kolb. Leiden: Brill.

Clark, Stuart. 1997. *Thinking with Demons: The Idea of Witchcraft in Early Modern Europe.* Oxford: Oxford University Press.

Clark, Stuart. 2007. *Vanities of the Eye: Vision in Early Modern European Culture.* Oxford: Oxford University Press.

Cohn, Norman. 1993. *Europe's Inner Demons: The Demonization of Christians in Medieval Christendom.* Chicago: University of Chicago Press.

Crowther-Heyck, Kathleen. 2002. "Be Fruitful and Multiply: Genesis and Generation in Reformation Germany." *Renaissance Quarterly* 55 (3): 904–35.

Crowther-Heyck, Kathleen. 2003. "Wonderful Secrets of Nature: Natural Knowledge and Religious Piety in Reformation Germany." *Isis* 94 (2): 253–73.

Crowther, Kathleen. 2010. *Adam and Eve in the Protestant Reformation.* Cambridge: Cambridge University Press.

Dingel, Irene. 2008. "The Culture of Conflict in the Controversies Leading to the Formula of Concord." In *Lutheran Ecclesiastical Culture, 1550–1675,* edited by Robert Kolb, 15–64. Leiden: Brill.

Dingel, Irene, ed. 2014. *Die Bekenntnisschriften der evangelisch-lutherischen Kirche.* Göttingen: Vandenhoeck und Ruprecht.

Duggan, Lawrence G. 1984. "Fear and Confession on the Eve of the Reformation." *Archiv Für Reformationsgeschichte – Archive for Reformation History* 75: 153–75.

Dunte, Ludovicus. 1664. *Decisiones mille et sex casuum conscientiae: Kurtze und richtige Erörterung/Tausend und Sechs gewissens Fragen/auff vielerley in theologischen Schulen/Predigampte/Und Consistorien fürfallenden Sachen und zutragenden wichtigen Fällen.* Lübeck: Wetstein.

Eire, Carlos M.N. 2005. "'Bite This, Satan!' The Devil in Luther's Table Talk." In *Piety and Family in Early Modern Europe: Essays in Honour of Steven Ozment,* edited by Marc C. Forster and Benjamin J. Kaplan, 70–93. Burlington, VT: Ashgate.

Frankfurter, David. 2010. "Where the Spirits Dwell: Possession, Christianization, and Saints' Shrines in Late Antiquity." *The Harvard Theological Review* 13 (1): 27–46.

Haeming, Mary Jane, and Robert Kolb. 2008. "Preaching in the Lutheran Pulpits in the Age of Confessionalization." In *Lutheran Ecclesiastical Culture, 1550–1675,* edited by Robert Kolb, 117–57. Leiden: Brill.

Hrotsvitha. 2001. *Hrotsvit: Opera Omnia.* Edited by Walther Berschin. Bibliotheca Scriptorvm Graecorvm et Romanorvm Tevbneriana. Munich: Saur.

Johnstone, Nathan. 2012. "The Protestant Devil: The Experience of Temptation in Early Modern England." *Journal of British Studies* 43 (2): 173–205.

Jost, Jean E. 2016a. "Spirituality in the Late Middle Ages: Affective Piety in the Pricke of Conscience H.M. 128." In *Death in the Middle Ages and Early Modern Times: The Material and Spiritual Conditions of the Culture of Death*, edited by Albrecht Classen, 387–405. Berlin: De Gruyter.

Jost, Jean E. 2016b. "The Effects of the Black Death: The Plague in Fourteenth-Century Religion, Literature, and Art." In *Death in the Middle Ages and Early Modern Times: The Material and Spiritual Conditions of the Culture of Death*, edited by Albrecht Classen, 193–237. Berlin: De Gruyter.

Karant-Nunn, Susan. 1997. *The Reformation of Ritual: An Interpretation of Early Modern Germany*. London: Routledge.

Karant-Nunn, Susan. 1998. "The Reformation of Women." In *Becoming Visible: Women in European History*, edited by Renate Bridenthal, Susan Mosher Stuard, and Merry E. Wiesner-Hanks. Boston: Houghton-Mifflin.

Kieckhefer, Richard. 1989. *Magic in the Middle Ages*. Cambridge: Cambridge University Press.

Klibansky, Raymond, Erwin Panofsky, and Fritz Saxl. 1979. *Saturn and Melancholy: Studies in the History of Natural Philosophy, Religion and Art*. Nedlen Liechtenstein: Kraus-Thomson.

Kolb, Robert. 1982. "God, Faith, and the Devil: Popular Lutheran Treatments of the First Commandment in the Era of the Book of Concord." *Fides et Historia* 15: 71–89.

Kolb, Robert. 2004. "The Braunschweig Resolution: The *Corpus Doctrinae Prutenicum* of Joachim Mörlin and Martin Chemnitz as an Interpretation of Wittenberg Theology." In *Confessionalization in Europe, 1555–1700: Essays in Honor and Memory of Bodo Nischan*, edited by John M. Headley, Hans J. Hillebrand, and Anthony J. Papalas, 67–89. Aldershot: Ashgate.

Kolb, Robert, and Timothy J. Wengert. 2000. *The Book of Concord: The Confessions of the Evangelical Lutheran Church*. Translated by Charles Arand. Minneapolis: Fortress Press.

Kruse, Gottschalk. 1522. *Van Adams und unsem Valle und wedder Upperstandinghe*. Braunschweig: Hans Dorn.

Kruse, Gottschalk. 1523. *To allen Christ gelövigen fromen mynschen beßondern der statt Brunswygk*. Wittenberg: Nickel Schirlentz.

Langbein, J.L. 1974. *Prosecuting Crime in the Renaissance: England, Germany and France*. Cambridge, MA: Harvard University Press.

Levack, Brian. 2006. *The Witch-Hunt in Early Modern Europe*. 3rd ed. Harlow: Pearson Education.

Levack, Brian. 2013. *The Devil Within: Possession and Exorcism in the Christian West*. New Haven: Yale University Press.

Lindberg, Carter. 2010. *The European Reformations*. 2nd ed. Chichester: Wiley & Sons.

Lohse, Bernhard. 2011. *Martin Luther's Theology: Its Historical and Systematic Development*. Minneapolis: Fortress Press.

Luther, Martin. 1518. *Eyn Sermon von dem Ablaß vnnd gnade*. Brunswick: Hans Dorn.

Luther, Martin. 1955–2016. *Luther's Works (American Edition)*. Edited by Jaroslav Pelikan and Hartmut Lehmann. 56 vols. Philadelphia and St. Louis: Muehlenberg, Fortress and Concord.

MacKay, Christopher S. 2009. *The Hammer of Witches: A Complete Translation of the Malleus Maleficarum*. Cambridge: Cambridge University Press.

Martin, Roderick. 2008. "The Reformation of Conscience: Rhetoric in the Lutheran Casuistry of Friedrich Balduin (1575–1627)." PhD Diss., University of Virginia.

Mayes, Benjamin T.G. 2016. "Friedrich Balduin (1575–1627)." In *Lives & Writings of the Great Fathers of the Lutheran Church*, edited by T. Schmeling, 97–112. St. Louis: Concordia Publishing House.

Mayes, Benjamin T.G. 2017. "Demon Possession and Exorcism in Lutheran Orthodoxy." *Concordia Theological Quarterly* 81 (3–4): 331–36.

McGrath, Alister E. 2012. *Reformation Thought: An Introduction*. 4th ed. Chichester: Wiley & Sons.

Midelfort, H.C. Erik. 1984. "Sin, Melancholy and Obsession: Insanity and Culture in Early Modern Germany." In *Understanding Popular Culture: Europe from the Middle Ages to the Nineteenth Century*, edited by Steven L. Kaplan, 113–45. Berlin: Walter de Gruyter.

Midelfort, H.C. Erik. 1988. "Johann Weyer and the Transformation of the Insanity Defence." In *The German People and the Reformation*, edited by Ronnie Po-chia Hsia, 266–78. Ithaca: Cornell University Press.

Midelfort, H.C. Erik. 1999. *A History of Madness in Sixteenth-Century Germany*. Stanford: Stanford University Press.

Midelfort, H.C. Erik. 2016. "Medicine, Theology, and the Problem of Germany's Pietist Ecstatics." In *God in the Enlightenment*, edited by William Bulman and Robert Ingram, 236–56. Oxford: Oxford University Press.

Mora, George, and Benjamin Kohl, eds. 1991. *Witches, Devils, and Doctors in the Renaissance: Johann Weyer, De Praestigiis Daemonum*. Translated by John Shea. Binghamton, NY: Medieval and Renaissance Texts and Studies.

Mörlin, Joachim. 1587. *Postilla: Oder summarische Erinnerung bey den sonteglichen Jahrs Evangelien und Catechismi*. Erfurt: Tröster.

Morton, Peter A. ed. 2017. *The Trial of Tempel Anneke: Records of a Witchcraft Trial in Brunswick, Germany, 1663*. Translated by Barbara Dähms. 2nd ed. Toronto: University of Toronto Press.

Morton, Peter A. 2018. "Superstition, Witchcraft and the First Commandment in the Late Middle Ages." *Magic, Ritual and Witchcraft* 13 (1): 40–70.

Musaeus, Simon. 1569. *Nützlicher Bericht, unnd heilsammer Rath aus Gottes Wort, wider den melancholischen Teuffel: Allen schwermütigen ... Hertzen, zum sonderlichen beschwerten Trost.* Nürnberg.

Musaeus, Simon. 1579. *Melancholischer Teufel, Nützlicher Bericht und heilsamer Rath ...Wie man alle melancholische, teuflische Gedancken, und sich trösten soll ...* Tham in der Newenmarck: Runge.

Myers, William David. 2011. *Death and a Maiden: Infanticide and the Tragical History of Grethe Schmidt.* DeKalb, IL: North Illinois University Press.

Neser, Johannes. 1617. *Drey christliche Predigten, die zwo Ersten, auß d. 77. Psalmen, von Melancholia, Schwermütigkeit ... die dritte Predigt: aus d. 88. Psalmen. von den erschrecklichen Anfechtungen der Verzweiffelung.* Wittenberg: Bormann.

Neukirch, Melchior. 1596a. *Andechtige christliche Gebete/Wider die Teuffel in den armen besessenen Leuten.: Der gottseligen Jungfrawen/Apollonien/ des erbarn Heinrich Stampken/Bürgers zu Braunschweig in S. Peters Pfarr wonhafftig/geliebten Tochter/welche vom leidigen Sathan/durch Gottes Verhengnuß leibhaftig besessen Ist/vnd von demselben grewlich geplaget wird/ zu Trost vnd christlicher Vbung gestellet/auff Begeren vieler frommen Christen zusammen gedruckt.* Helmstedt: Jacob Lucius.

Neukirch, Melchior. 1596b. *Die tröstliche Historia Lazari aus/Dem eilften Capittel Johannes/in neun Predigten gefasset/und erkleret.* Helmstedt: Jacob Lucius.

Newman, Barbara. 1998. "Possessed by the Spirit: Devout Women, Demoniacs, and the Apostolic Life in the Thirteenth Century." *Speculum* 73 (3): 733–70.

Oberman, Heiko A. 1973. "The Shape of Late Medieval Thought: The Birthpangs of the Modern Era." *Archiv Für Reformationsgeschichte – Archive for Reformation History* 64 (December): 13–33.

Ozment, Steven E. 1975. *The Reformation in the Cities: The Appeal of Protestantism to Sixteenth-Century Germany and Switzerland.* New Haven, CT: Yale University Press.

Ozment, Steven E. 1980. *The Age of Reform (1250–1550): An Intellectual and Religious History of Late Medieval and Reformation Europe.* New Haven: Yale University Press.

Ozment, Steven E. 1983. *When Fathers Ruled: Family Life in Reformation Europe.* Cambridge, MA: Harvard University Press.

Peters, Edward. 2001. "The Medieval Church and State on Superstition, Magic, and Witchcraft from Augustine to the Sixteenth Century." In *The*

History of Witchcraft in Europe: The Middle Ages, edited by Bengt Ankarloo and Stuart Clark, 173–245. London: Athlone Press.

Plummer, Marjorie Elizabeth. 1996. "Reforming the Family: Marriage, Gender and the Lutheran Household in Early Modern Germany, 1500–1620." PhD Diss., University of Virginia.

Price, David H., ed. 2015. *The Works of Hrotsvit of Gandersheim: Facsimile of the First Edition (1501)*. Women in Print 2. Champaign: University of Illinois.

Raber, Karen, ed. 2013. *A Cultural History of Women in the Renaissance*. A Cultural History of Women 3. London: Bloomsbury Academic.

Raiswell, Richard, and Peter Dendle. 2008. "Demon Possession in Anglo-Saxon and Early Modern England: Continuity and Evolution in Social Context." *Journal of British Studies* 47 (4): 738–67.

Read, Sara. 2015. *Maids, Wives, Widows: Exploring Early Modern Women's Lives, 1540–1740*. Barnsley: Pen & Sword Books.

Reinburg, Virginia. 1992. "Liturgy and the Laity in Late Medieval and Reformation France." *The Sixteenth Century Journal* 23 (3): 526–47.

Riedl, Peter Phillipp. 2006. *Historia von D. Johann Fausti: Kritische Ausgabe der jüngeren Version von 1589*. Berlin: Weidler.

Roper, Lyndal. 1991. *The Holy Household: Women and Morals in Reformation Augsburg*. Oxford: Clarendon Press.

Scaer, David P. 1983. "The Concept of Anfechtung in Luther's Thought." *Concordia Theological Quarterly* 47 (1): 15–30.

Schleiner, Winfried. 1991. *Melancholy, Genius, and Utopia in the Renaissance*. Wolfenbuetteler Arbeitskreis Zur Renaissanceforschung. Wiesbaden: Harrassovitz.

Schroeder, Friedrich-Christian, ed. 2000. *Die peinliche Gerichtsordnung Kaiser Karls V. und des heiligen römischen Reichs*. Universal-Bibliothek. Stuttgart: Reclam.

Scribner, Robert W. 1987a. *Popular Culture and Popular Movements in Reformation Germany*. London and Ronceverte: Hambledon Press.

Scribner, Robert W. 1987b. "Cosmic Order and Daily Life: Sacred and Secular in Pre-Industrial German Society." In *Popular Culture and Popular Movements in Reformation Germany*, 1–16. London: Hambledon Press.

Scribner, Robert W. 1988. "Ritual and Reformation." In *The German People and the Reformation*, edited by Ronnie Po-chia Hsia, 122–44. Ithaca: Cornell University Press.

Scribner, Robert W. 2011. *Religion and Culture in Germany (1400–1800)*. Edited by Lyndal Roper. Leiden: Brill.

Seifert, Wolfgang S. 1952. "The Concept of the Devil and the Myth of the Pact in Literature Prior to Goethe." *Monatshefte* 44 (6): 271–89.

Shantz, Douglas H. 2013. *An Introduction to German Pietism: Protestant Renewal at the Dawn of Modern Europe.* Baltimore: Johns Hopkins University Press.

Shantz, Douglas H, ed. 2015. *A Companion to German Pietism, 1660–1800.* Leiden: Brill.

Slattery, Joseph A. 1979. "The Catechetical Use of the Decalogue from the End of the Catechumenate through the Late Medieval Period." PhD Diss., Catholic University of America.

Sluhovsky, Moshe. 1996. "A Divine Apparition or Demonic Possession? Female Agency and Church Authority in Demonic Possession in Sixteenth-Century France." *The Sixteenth Century Journal* 27 (4): 1039–55.

Spiess, Werner. 1966. *Geschichte der Stadt Braunschweig im Nachmittelalter: Vom Ausgang des Mittelalters bis zum Ende der Stadtfreiheit (1491–1671).* 2 vols. Braunschweig: Waisenhaus.

Spiess, Werner. 1970. *Die Ratsherren der Hansestadt Braunschweig 1231–1671.* Braunschweig: Waisenhaus.

Der Stadt Braunschweig Ordnunge jre christliche Religion auch allerhandt Criminal Straff vnd Policey-Sachen betreffendt. Reprint der Orig.-Ausg. von 1579. 2002. Braunschweig: Archiv-Verlag.

Stitziel, Judd. 1996. "God, the Devil, Medicine, and the Word: A Controversy over Ecstatic Women in Protestant Middle Germany, 1691–1693." *Central European History* 29: 309–37.

Strauss, Gerald. 1978. *Luther's House of Learning: Indoctrination of the Young in the German Reformation.* Baltimore: Johns Hopkins University Press.

Tamm, Marek. 2003. "Saints and the Demoniacs: Exorcistic Rites in Medieval Europe (11th–13th Century)." *Folklore* 23: 7–24. https://doi.org/doi:10.7592/FEJF2003.23.exorcism.

Tappert, Theodore G. 1959. *The Book of Concord: The Confessions of the Evangelical Lutheran Church.* Philadelphia: Fortress Press.

Tentler, Thomas N. 1977. *Sin and Confession on the Eve of the Reformation.* Princeton, NJ: Princeton University Press.

Wailes, Stephen L. 2006. *Spirituality and Politics in the Works of Hrotsvit of Gandersheim.* Selinsgrove: Susquehanna University Press.

Wandel, Lee Palmer. 2015. *Reading Catechisms, Teaching Religion.* Brill's Studies on Art, Art History, and Intellectual History. Leiden: Brill Academic Publishers.

Wiegand, Gonsalva. 1936. "The Non-Dramatic Works of Hrotsvitha: Text, Translation and Commentary." Saint Louis: Saint Louis University.

Wiesner, Merry E. 1993. *Women and Gender in Early Modern Europe.* Cambridge: Cambridge University Press.

Wiesner-Hanks, Merry E. 2006. "Women, Gender and Sexuality." In *Palgrave Advances in the European Reformations*, edited by Alec Ryrie, 253–72. London: Palgrave MacMillan.

Wilde, Manfred. 2003. *Die Zauberei- und Hexenprozesse in Kursachsen.* Cologne: Böhlau.

Wiltenburg, Joy. 2000. "The Carolina and the Culture of the Common Man: Revisiting the Imperial Penal Code of 1532." *Renaissance Quarterly* 53 (3): 713–34.

Zell, Katharina. 2006. *Church Mother: The Writings of a Protestant Reformer in Sixteenth-Century Germany.* Translated by Elise Ann McKee. Chicago: University of Chicago Press.

Sources

We gratefully acknowledge permission from the Städtisches Museum Braunschweig to reproduce Figures 4 and 5.

Friedrich Bernhard Werner (1690–1778), *Gesamtansicht der Stadt Braunschweig (von Osten und Norden)*. Printed by Jeremias Wolff Erben, Augsburg, 1729, copper engraving, colored, 34.5 × 104 cm (h × w), Städtisches Museum Braunschweig, Inv.-No. 1600-2629-00. © Städtisches Museum Braunschweig, Photograph: Jakob Adolphi.

Anton August Beck (1713–1787), *Das Neustadtrathaus in Braunschweig von Nordosten vor dem Umbau 1773*. Eighteenth century, pen and ink and colored pencil, Städtisches Museum Braunschweig, no inventory number. © Städtisches Museum Braunschweig, Photograph: Dirk Scherer.

We gratefully acknowledge permission from the Stadtarchiv Braunschweig to reproduce Figures 6, 7, 8, 9, and 10.

Interrogatoria praeliminaria worüber Catharine Lorenzin zu vernehmen, 24.12.1667. (Stadtarchiv Braunschweig B IV 15b Nr 32, Blatt 15r).

H. Physici D. Laurentii Gieselers bericht. (Stadtarchiv Braunschweig B IV 15b Nr 32, Blatt 33r).

Decanus, Senior undt andere Doctores der Juristen Facultät [Helmstedt] daselbst, 11.2.1668. (Stadtarchiv Braunschweig B IV 15b Nr 32, Blatt 49v).

Actum Fronerey Newstadt, 12.3.1668. (Stadtarchiv Braunschweig B IV 15b Nr 32, Blatt 50r).

Dismissio Elisabethen Lorentzin betr, 12.3.1668. (Stadtarchiv Braunschweig B IV 15b Nr 32, Blatt 51r).

We gratefully acknowledge permission from the Herzog August Bibliothek to reproduce Figure 11.

Herzog August Bibliothek Wolfenbüttel: 918.2 Theol. (8). Melchior Neukirch, *Andechtige Christliche gebete wider die Teuffel in den armen besessenen leuten* (Helmstedt: Lucius, 1596), Title page.

Index